BE A SUCCESSFUL WRITER
99 **SUREFIRE** CHECKLISTS

Other Allison & Busby Writers' Guides by Gordon Wells

The Magazine Writer's Handbook
The Book Writer's Handbook
The Craft of Writing Articles
The Business of Writing
Writers' Questions Answered
Photography for Article-Writers
The Best of Writers' Monthly

BE A SUCCESSFUL WRITER

99 **SUREFIRE** CHECKLISTS

Gordon Wells

First published in Great Britain in 1999 by
Allison & Busby Ltd
114 New Cavendish Street
London W1M 7FD
http://www.allisonandbusby.ltd.uk

A catalogue record for this book is available from
the British Library.

ISBN 0 7490 0348 0

Typeset by DAG Publications Ltd, London.
Printed and bound in Great Britain by
Biddles Ltd, Guildford.

CONTENTS

the likely readership of a non-fiction book. Children's non-fiction book ideas.

INTRODUCTION
and Acknowledgements

As a 'how-to' book for writers, this one is different. It deals with a wide range of writing matters in the most concise way. It has been designed and organised not only as a general step-by-step guide for the beginner but also as a dip-in memory jogger for the established writer.

In the business management world it has long been accepted that bullet-point lists are a highly effective way of conveying essential information. I have adopted this practice in this book. Whatever you're working on, whoever you are, it should be worth having a quick look at the relevant checklist. We are all prone to forget things. Indeed, had I worked purely from memory in preparing the lists they would all have been far shorter – and less helpful.

I have tried to make each of the checklists complete in themselves. Inevitably, this means a certain amount of overlap and repetition. Where possible, without inconveniencing the reader, I have reduced the overlap by cross-referencing. For some, where my own experience is more limited than I would like, I have drawn heavily on the published advice of others – particularly Jean Saunders, Stella Whitelaw and Chriss McCallum – to whom I am most grateful. My special thanks too, to Jean Saunders for check-reading the first draft and picking up some of my faults. Irrespective of sources and checks though, any residual errors are of course down to me.

Several of the checklists have already appeared in the specialist writing magazines: some in *Writers' Monthly*, usually as conventional 'joined-up' feature articles, and some in *Writers' Forum*, where the checklist format proved particularly popular. These are gratefully identified throughout by the 'WM' or 'WF' at the end of the checklists – most of which have been amended somewhat since their initial publication.

1

GETTING STARTED

- **Breaking your duck**

- **Fillers**

- **Writing picture-stories (picture-script)**

- **Competitions**

- **Writing habits**

- **'Five-finger exercises'**

- **A writer's journal/notebook**

- **Starting a scrapbook**

- **Writing pitfalls**

- **Tips from the top**

- **Try something different**

- **How long is a piece of string?**

1 Breaking your duck

Every novice writer needs to get something published (for payment). That first published piece generates an enormous *ego* boost. It doesn't really matter WHAT the beginner gets published. They just need something to show to others, to prove they really are writers. This checklist of different ideas should help to get you into print.

- When next in the supermarket, forget the shelves: watch the people. Watch out for strange – or even better, amusing –

behaviour. Write a reader's letter to a (paying) editor about it.

- Mingle with the mothers waiting outside the local primary school at the end of school. Listen to them – and the kids. Someone's almost bound to say something interesting, amusing or just 'cute'. Report what you overhear to 'Out of the Mouths of Babes ...' columns – or, again, the letters page.

- Think carefully just how you do your everyday chores. Do you do anything in an unusual, more effective way? Write it up – BRIEFLY – as a hint. Several magazines pay for such advice.

- Choose with care the magazine to which you send your letter, kiddicomment or hint. Study the published letters, hints, etc. – length, style, etc. – and model your first submissions on these. (That's good practice for the market study you will need to do throughout your writing life.) Choose the magazine that pays best for everything they use. (Star prizes are 'chancy' when you're starting.)

- If you find it hard to write in the brief, cheerful style favoured by letters page editors, try a 'conventional' article for your county magazine. Research and write a history of some LITTLE-KNOWN local building, statue or historical figure. The pay's small but so is the competition. And, as always, study how the magazine likes such pieces, before writing.

- If you're really more into fiction than reporting real life, concentrate, for a while on, for example, the D. C. Thomson magazines. They pay less than others – which means less competition and therefore more chance of success – and the editorial people are ever helpful if you're 'nearly there'.

- Another area for a budding fiction writer to 'break a duck' is picture-story scripts (see Checklist Number 3). Again, look at D. C. Thomson comics and send them a script for one of the regular, preferably one-page, characters. (DCT 'own' most of the characters: anyone can write about them – but only, of course, for DCT.) And no, you don't have to draw the pix – just describe them; and write the dialogue.

- Even poets – for whom getting into print is always difficult – can 'break their duck' by writing shorter, more popular, pieces. Several women's magazines publish occasional poems as page-end fillers. Such poems need to be 'conventional' – with rhyme and metre – and SHORT (a dozen lines good, half a dozen better).

- Another possibility for getting poetry published is in greetings cards. Here, it's got to be either 'old-fashioned-slush' or 'modern-naughty-wit', in 'conventional-style', and even shorter – four short lines is a good target. And again, study the market before submission: browse through the cards in the racks – and take note of the publishers.

● It is also occasionally possible to get a short poem published as a Reader's Letter. For such use the poem needs a clear, relevant, message – expressed 'conventionally'.

[WF]

2 Fillers

A filler is a short piece of writing – from, say, 25 words, up to about 300 or 400. Its name more or less explains its purpose: fillers are used by magazine editors to fill in the small spaces left at the page-ends of stories and articles. There is a seemingly never-ending demand for them. Review your own experiences, expertise and memory – you probably have the material for a few fillers already at your fingertips. And you can always listen out for, read up on, or devise more. Fillers can be:

● anecdotes – humour is good but not essential. What **IS** essential is that they be entertaining and/or interest-grabbing.
● hints and tips on how to do everyday (and/or occasional) chores better, more effectively.
● how you solved some personal or family problem – slanted as advice on how the reader can do likewise.
● a religious (or other) 'Thought for the Day/Week/Month'.
● an interesting or humorous quotation, relevant to the target magazine, from a famous person, or a small, related batch of such quotes. (Peruse dictionaries of quotations – and today's newspapers. Don't worry about copyright – so long as the quote is brief.)
● a joke – but avoid shaggy dogs. Keep 'em short and punchy. Some magazines even welcome 'reported' jokes – heard on radio or TV.
● a market-relevant thought-provoking problem/puzzle – but only if the answer is brief. (A dozen words at most – and a single word is better still. A puzzle filler is fine: finding nearby space for the answer may be difficult.)
● entertaining news items (including 'boobs', misprints, badly-worded classified ads, etc.) 'found' in local newspapers, etc., are worth reporting to various national publications.
● a small collection of 'fractured sayings' – e.g., *a stitch in time saves later embarrassment*. (Collected one-liners of any type are

11

particularly useful because the editor can trim the resultant filler to fit the space to be filled.)

● a few subject-related little-known facts presented as a series of linked sentences in one paragraph, e.g.,

Tea, our national drink, was only introduced to Britain in 1657; before that, much weak wine and beer was drunk. When first sold in Britain, tea was brewed in bulk, stored in casks, drawn off when required and heated up. Sounds ghastly. But they must have improved the taste a lot, for, by 1675 King Charles I banned the sale of tea from private houses: he thought they were 'centres of sedition and intrigue'.

The well-known, world-circulating *Reader's Digest* has used page-end fillers for many years in such series as 'Life's Like That' and 'Humour in Uniform'. Their fillers are seldom longer than 100 words (although they like to edit them down from maybe 300 words) for which they pay about £1 *per word* and up.

Note: Alison Chisholm's *How to Write Five-Minute Features* (Allison & Busby) includes excellent advice on writing letters and various types of filler.

3 Writing picture-stories (picture-script)

Picture-stories – as found in comics, American magazines and full-length 'graphic novels' – can be a good way for a novice writer to get started. Graphic novels of course, need prior experience in the genre, but one- to three-page stories for weekly comics could be within the capability of many new writers.

To make a start, some pointers:

● The writer doesn't have to draw the pictures – and indeed, should be positively discouraged from attempting this.
● The characters in most comic magazine picture-stories are the 'copyright property' of the magazine's publisher. Many – but not all – of the characters are therefore open to freelance contributions. This means that – subject to prior checking with the editor – a freelance writer may produce a picture-story about a regular character in a specific magazine but may then only offer the story to that magazine.

- Picture-stories are told in a (relatively) fixed number of pictures, known as frames or panels. Most magazine picture-stories cover one, two or three pages. The number of frames per page can vary from about six to ten or twelve – different magazines adopting different numbers of frames per page. (Picture-stories for younger children usually have a smaller number of frames per page than do stories for older children.) You need to check the requirements for specific characters and magazines.
- The stories told in the pictures are like any other short story for children. You need a strong story about believable and consistent characters – which means prior study of their earlier stories – with plenty of action, plenty of conflict, and usually, plenty of humour. Avoid using too many (extra) characters and/or overcomplex settings. (Some picture-stories – such as romances for young girls – are told in photographs. For such scripts, in order that they remain cost-effective, firmly restrict the number of characters and do not specify 'impossible' locales.)
- Each frame (i.e., picture) is a snap-shot of an important moment in the ongoing action. You cannot show everything that happens – the readers, guided by the script-writer, use their own imagination to fill in what is happening in the inevitable gaps between the pictures. It is the (first) task of the writer to select the important moments in the story to be portrayed in each frame. The picture-script writer has to think visually.
- For each frame in a picture-story, the writer has to describe the scene such that the artist can draw it. (Different writer-artist teams may operate on different degrees of guidance being offered to the artist. This is usually a matter for editorial decision.)
- There is no scope for written description within the finished frame – only limited dialogue, thoughts, and sometimes, caption material, all of which has to be provided by the writer. (In most magazine picture-stories the within-frame caption material is usually restricted to brief comments to move the story along, such as 'Next morning,' or, 'Meanwhile'. In some book-length picture-stories the captions are longer. In many magazine picture-stories for very young children the captions – and essential dialogue – are wholly outside the frame.)
- As a rule of thumb, the total wordage – any caption plus not more than two speeches – within a frame is usually best restricted to about 25 words. (It is seldom practicable – for space reasons if no other – to include two separate speeches from a single character in any one frame. All dialogue should be kept as simple as possible.

And, as with all short stories, it should not only (seem to) be realistic but it also should always move the story forward – there's no room for lightweight chitchat.

- The 'viewpoint' in a picture-story is exclusively that of the artist (and the reader) – think of it as akin to a camera viewpoint. In this context, it is possible to suggest close-up, 'normal' or long-distance 'shots' and either worm's or bird's eye-view. Frames showing immobile 'talking heads' should as far as possible be restricted; at least vary the viewpoint – from behind or near alternate heads.

- Both speech and thoughts can be included in story-frames. (Speeches are in balloons, thoughts are in bubbles.) These artistic conventions are not the concern of the writer – who merely has to say 'Character C (THKS):'. Flashbacks can also occasionally be used (usually only in longer-length picture-stories); the artistic convention is a wavy edge to the frame; the writer merely specifies a particular frame as FLASHBACK.

- Picture-story scripts are set out in double-spaced typescript, as hanging paragraphs – effectively as two columns – usually with just two frames per A4 page. The script for each frame includes: frame number on left with scene description on right; the word 'Caption' on left, with wording on right; each active character's name on left with speech (or thoughts – identified) on right.

- Publishers often insist on buying 'All Rights' in a picture-story script – and seldom give the writer a by-line. (If you don't like the heat, stay out of the kitchen.)

Note: There is much detailed advice on scripting in Dave Taylor's picture-strip book, *A Guide to Comicscripting* (Robert Hale).

4 Competitions

Competitions are often a way for previously unpublished writers to get into print – and in many cases, even if they are unsuccessful, to get a helpful criticism of their work. But competitions need to be taken seriously. They all have rules ...

- Let's say the competition is for a short story: are you submitting an article, or part of that novel you're writing and of which you would like a *crit*? Or vice versa? The judges won't mind; you'll still get your *crit*. Oh, no you won't.

- The rules call for an 800-word entry: don't worry, your 2,500-word piece is not much longer – the judges won't mind. Oh, yes they will. (This principle is equally applicable in reverse. Don't submit an 800-word entry for a 2,500-word competition – unless the rules say, 'Up to 2,500 words ...')
- The rules call for an 800-word piece. Halfway through writing it, you realise you're going to need 2,500 words to get it all in ... so you cut the second half short and cover the remaining points in note form. The judges will understand. After all, you've kept it to length. Oh, no they won't. (You've ruined it. You need an 800-word subject/plot for an 800-word article/story.)
- The deadline for the competition is nigh. So you type the entry in a hurry –with several typing mistakes. Corrected in ink, your entry looks a mess. The judges won't mind. Oh, yes they will. Retype it.
- Again on presentation: competition entries should always be well presented, with good wide margins, double-spaced typescript and consistent paragraph indents. Variation from that norm will make your entry look more 'interesting'. The judges will enjoy it. Oh, no they won't.
- Because of the rush to meet the deadline, you don't have time to reread your entry: you have neither found nor corrected your spelling mistakes and typos. The judges won't notice or mind. Oh, yes they will.
- The competition is for an article; you are required to state the magazine for which it was written. You consider this a silly requirement – it's suitable for any magazine. So you either don't specify the market or specify one that doesn't accept contributions. The judges won't mind – they probably don't know much about potential markets anyway. Oh, yes they will – and they do.
- It's past the closing date. The judges won't mind, they'll still consider your entry. Oh, yes they will, and no they won't.
- To summarise – comply with the rules, or don't enter.

[WF]

5 Writing habits

- Do you believe in yourself as a writer, and in your work? If you think of your work as amateur scribblings, why should you expect an editor to buy it? And if you're not writing with the hope of publication, what on earth are you doing it for? You've got to believe that you have talent, that if you work hard and regularly at your writing, you WILL get published. You've got to have a good *attitude*.

- Do you write something – no matter how little, but the more the better – every day, and preferably at more or less the same time? (You need to keep your 'writing muscle' in trim: without exercise it goes flabby – you forget how to do it.)
- Do you read back, to yourself – aloud – what you've written? With non-fiction and with descriptive passages in fiction, this is the way to identify pompous or over-wordy phrases; with dialogue it helps to ensure realism. (Make sure too that the dialogue moves the story forward.)
- Does your writing *flow*? You will often need to use short, simple sentences but make sure they're not (unintentionally) jumpy – and remember to add in, or retain, link words at the beginning of paragraphs, etc.
- Do you stop work when the scene you are writing begins to feel boring, when you're tired of writing it and can't wait to get it over and done with? You should – if it's boring you, think what it's doing for the readers.
- When you finish work at the end of a (daily) session, have you tried stopping in mid-sentence or mid-scene, to ease the next-day's start-up? (I sometimes go further: I stop typing in mid-sentence but complete the sentence in pencil – plus notes of what's to follow; next day, I can then start straight away, typing the pencilled-in words. That usually gets me going.)
- Do you make a last-minute check of your ready-to-go-off work ... for the overlooked typos, for spelling errors, for unwanted extra spaces, etc.? Correct them before the work goes off – the editor will think better of you if your work is perfect in this respect.
- How long do you sit basking in the glow of having completed and sent off a story, article or book, before you start thinking about the next one? A couple of days is plenty. The professional writer will always try to have the next project in mind before the first is complete: it's not always possible but the principle is right – keep at it. (Back to *attitude* again.)
- Are you generally businesslike in your writing activities – keeping a record of submissions, and checks on payments due, etc.? (See Checklists 94–95.)

[WF]

6 'Five-finger exercises'

Musicians loosen up by playing scales and other exercises: beginner pianists learn special 'five-finger exercises' to get used to the keyboard. Writing teachers often recommend similar exercises to get wannabe writers into a creative mood. Some of the exercises are worth repeating, even when you are past the initial wannabe stage – they help to keep the writing muscles flexible and active. Try these out:

- Think of someone you know. In about 300 words, describe them, both physically and characteristically, as though to someone who doesn't know them.
- Again, in about 300 words, describe the scene outside your 'writing room' window. Restrict your description to what can be seen within the bounds of the frame, without moving your head.
- Rewrite/edit either or both the above two descriptions – using no adverbs or adjectives at all. Then indulge yourself – add just one 'luxury' adjective into each description.
- Repeat the first exercise, describing another acquaintance who, to the best of your knowledge, doesn't know the first one.
- Again, in about 300 words, let your two characters meet ... and have a row. Write the dialogue only, with virtually no description.
- Write a *haiku*. Five syllables in line one, seven in line two, and five in line three. A *haiku* should 'encapsulate an element of a season and evoke a mood', advises Alison Chisholm in her *The Craft of Writing Poetry* (Allison & Busby). No rhyme is necessary but the third line should be a comment on the first two. If an old hack like me could write one – and I have – so can you, even if you're no poet.
- Try writing a complete story in 50 words, not counting the title – and make sure the story has a beginning, a middle and an end.

7 A writer's journal/notebook

Every writer should have a notebook. It may be used as a daily journal (an actual diary will seldom be sufficiently flexible or spacious) or as a place to jot down all sorts of important things whenever required – which will usually end up as daily.

Remember: your 'writing life' is going to go into your notebook. Find yourself a book with which you will be happy and comfortable – hardback or softback, decorative or businesslike, bound or loose-leaf, large or small, lined or unlined pages – even lockable, if that makes you feel better. Think whether you wish to take your notebook everywhere with you – often a good idea, but this will certainly influ-

17

ence your choice of size. (Alternatives to consider are carrying a few loose-leaf pages with you, for later filing in the main binder, or carrying a small book with you and copying out notes each evening into the 'notebook proper' – or just a big handbag/briefcase.) Over a lifetime, you may well accumulate many volumes of your notebook: consistency of appearance will look good on your bookshelf.

Now, what to put in it:

- Spend a few minutes each day to review the last twenty-four hours. Make a note of happenings that might be of later use/interest – and don't forget your feelings and innermost thoughts too.
- Throughout your day, keep alert for interesting overheard comments or conversation, unusual snippets of information, even an interesting occurrence – make a note of them as soon as possible.
- Whenever an idea – for an article, short story or book-scene – comes to you, make a note of it. Ideas are notoriously ephemeral.
- Make a note, describing any interesting – or ordinary – people you come across during your daily round. Your notes will be invaluable later, when you have to describe a fictional character.
- And ... anything else you like.

About once a week, read through your notebook: think about what you've noted down. Some notes will be immediately useful; others may be best left to mature. **NEVER** THROW ANYTHING OUT – ONE DAY YOU'LL *NEED* THAT 'RUBBISH' ENTRY.

8 Starting a scrapbook

As soon as you get anything published – a (preferably, but not necessarily, paid-for) letter or hint, even an unpaid article in a small press magazine – you should start a scrapbook. (I've got literally dozens of them, stretching back years.) If you neglect starting one as soon as anything is published, one day you'll kick yourself.

Your scrapbook is your 'prize cabinet', your 'mounted heads on the wall'. It will serve at least two other purposes: to lift your spirits at moments of depression, when everything is getting rejected; and to provide an immediate, and reliable research source for future work.

You can use either a 'traditional' type of scrapbook, obtainable for a pound or so from everybody's favourite multiple stationers, or use loose-leaf binders holding hole-punched plastic sleeves. The latter approach allows removal of cuttings, etc., for ease of photocopying, but there will occasionally be items too big to be accommodated, and there is always the possibility of removing cuttings and neglecting to replace them. With plastic sleeves, stick small cuttings on blank A4 sheets before 'sleeving'.

Into your scrapbook, put:

- published letters, fillers, etc. – whether paid for or not.
- published articles – in whatever publication, small press magazine or national daily. (If you sell a series, keep them all together, possibly in a dedicated scrapbook.)
- published short stories – ditto.
- published poems – even limericks, greetings cards, etc.
- programmes of events at which you speak.
- extra copies ('pulls') of the covers of your books.
- the listing of your book in the publisher's catalogue and/or advertisements.
- the advance information (AI) sheets for each of your books.
- press releases relating to your books.
- press cuttings of reviews of your books.
- press cuttings of news items about you and your writing activities.

Make sure that each cutting, etc., going into your scrapbook is dated and its source identified.

9 Writing pitfalls

None of us is perfect; from time to time we all fall into one or more of the writing pitfalls that regularly confront us. Check your own practices against this list – and then try the suggestions of how to overcome them:

- **Irrelevance**. Are you sticking to the point of your article? Or have you introduced a second subject into your initial article-topic? If you attempt to ride two horses, or even change from one to t'other, in mid-stream – you can easily fall off and get a soaking. It helps, I find, to scribble the subject, or the objective, of an article at the head of the sheet of paper on which I make my initial plan. That keeps me on track.
   Storytellers too can fall into the pit of irrelevance. Are you

19

diverging from the plot of your story? A sub-plot may be necessary in a novel – but seldom in a short story. It is usually an irrelevance.

Have you introduced an irrelevant character? Several minor characters can often be 'combined' into just one. Short stories, particularly, should have short cast lists.

- **Laziness**. Are you skimping on the rewriting and polishing of your work? Or even neglecting your writing for a day or so *without good reason*. That's laziness. Unless you overcome laziness, you'll never make it as a writer. You'll remain a wannabe. Along with all the others.

- **Insufficient or inaccurate information**. Are you not bothering to do enough research? Research is an essential for every writer. You need to KNOW the name of that street in eighteenth century Santa Delbrovnika along which your lovesick hero is picking his weary way home in the small hours. You need to KNOW the year in which *procalciophyacine* was discovered. (I'm playing safe: I've invented both town and 'medicine'.)

  Yes, you can omit, and then write around the facts, i.e., *fudge* it. And omission is always a safe solution. But omit too much, fudge too often, and your story or article will lose the feel of truth. Guessing won't do, either. Include just one, tiny, unimportant, inconsequential, incorrect statement in your article, book or story, and some reader, somewhere, will catch you out. You may be damned for evermore.

  Remember though, there's another side to the coin. As an American writer once said – paraphrased, for the more delicate readers – research is like manure: spread thin it does wonders, but avoid the large dollops.

- **Overwriting** (waffling). We all, on occasions, write at greater length than necessary. We go too much with the flow. The published writer recognises this and trims it back when polishing.

  (Commenting on her own writing technique, best-selling author/TV playwright Lynda La Plante said, 'I just let the story travel. When that's done though, I edit – cut, cut, cut, cut, cut ...' Publishers say that nearly all book submissions – fiction or non-fiction – would be improved by a 10 per cent cut.)

  Identify the waffle by reading aloud. That will also flush out the pompous and stilted bits. Cut 'em all out.

When working to a set wordage, try writing about 20 per cent too much; then cut back. The improvement is staggering.

- **Opinionated writing**. Are you preaching? If so, get thee to a pulpit ... or a soapbox. Brutally, readers are most unlikely to be interested in *your* views on anything.

  If you can incorporate a character in your story who can expound your views, so be it. But don't shoehorn a character in, just to preach. The character's views and personality must fit together.

  Apart from a few 'Viewpoint' or 'My Pet Hate' spots, preaching opportunities are non-existent in the general-interest magazine press – preaching is a guaranteed rejection formula.

- **Stilted writing**. Have you been obfuscating – rather than being colloquial – in your writing? Popular writing has to be lively to succeed. Have you been using the passive, rather than the active voice? The passive voice is at the root of much dull writing.

  In its worst state, stilted non-fiction writing in the passive voice will sound like a Government Circular or White Paper. Incomprehensible. Solution: think active, avoid the passive voice whenever possible.

  In fiction, contrived and hackneyed plots and/or cardboard characters produce stilted writing.

  Cardboard characters are the ones which you can't picture or identify with. Real people are rounded personalities, complete with warts – nicotine-stained fingers, a permanent, deep-furrowed frown, a limp, a quick temper ... and so on. Real people are multi-coloured – not black and white – and cannot be adequately described in a few short words. Lift your characters out of the stilted ruck.

- **Inhibitions**. Have you fought shy of expressing emotions that might shock or surprise your friends, etc.? Some stories *demand* uninhibited descriptions of sensual feelings, emotions and activities. If your story needs it: write it. Make it come alive for your readers.

- **Poor sequencing**. Does your writing *flow*? This will be partly a product of your choice of words. Using 'link words' to start the next paragraph will help the flow, as will a simple writing style. But these are specifics.

Jumpy construction, that is, poor sequencing is often a greater hindrance to the flow. The inherent structure of an article is an equally important element. (See Checklist 38.)

The structure of a story too is most important: do you need that flashback, have you started the story at 'the right moment', have you resolved all the problems and conflicts?

- **Excessive reality**. Is your story too much like real life – don't tell me, on which it is based? Have you stuck too closely to 'what actually happened'? Real life is random, real life is dull, real life meanders on, slowly getting to the crunch. Fiction is different – fiction has to be exciting, fiction has to be unpredictable, fiction has to have a gripping beginning, a middle and a *satisfying* end.

  If you are writing an autobiography or a personal experience article the same principles apply. The truth, the whole truth and nothing but the truth may be necessary in law – but not in general interest writing. Be selective. Gloss over some matters and elaborate on others for a better read. Apply fictional techniques to tell a true story better.

[WM]

10 Tips from the top

Over the last few years in 'the writing business', I have asked many well-known authors for their advice for beginners. One way or another, just about everyone echoed Guy de Maupassant's 'Get black on white' advice – i.e., 'write, write, write'. Some of the other helpful suggestions from these writers – all very successful in their own fields – are:

- Laziness, impatience and conceit are the mortal enemies of the would-be writer. It's a jungle out there, a buyers' market for fiction, tougher than ever before. Publication is not going to come easy. Dedication and a clear-eyed realisation that good writing is a *craft* to be learned like any other will at least get you to the starting line.   – Jessica Stirling
- Self-criticism is the only way to improve your writing. Submit and resubmit your work. Nothing sells if it's in a cupboard. Never give up.   – Tessa Barclay
- Always write what you want to write because then you will do your best work. Don't let agents and/or publishers dominate you.

Remember, they would not exist without writers. Be immensely critical of your work. Cut, and prune, and cut again.

– Frederick E. Smith

● Never be afraid to learn from others. Listen – and care. Love what you do, even though it may hurt you. Never give up. Keep an open and subjective mind; be honourable to yourself and take pride in what you – only you, your mind and imagination – can do.

– Lynda La Plante

● Write about the world you know. Realise that you have a great influence upon your reader. You must try to give your reader happiness, good sense, and a belief in true love, which is what all men and women have sought since the beginning of civilisation.

– Barbara Cartland

● Too much revision can take the life and soul out of your work. Very often your white-hot writing is the most sparkling of all. It's your voice that must come through on the page. Above all, believe in yourself, act on any editorial help you get, and never give up.

– Jean Saunders

● Fill yourself up before you try to fill up a book. And don't listen to the advice of other writers. None of us really know how we made it. – Terry Pratchett

● Write daily and routinely to targets. Keep your ambition to yourself. Don't use others to give you moral support. Avoid displacement activities. – William Horwood

● Don't imagine that because you write you are unique. You are not. Writing is a very competitive field. What opportunities for success there are will be clamoured after. Drop pretension. So long as you believe in yourself and are willing to take the knocks and keep at it, then all will be fine. – Peter Finch

11 Try something different

There is more to the writing business/game than articles, short stories and books (novels or non-fiction). Any time you feel depressed due to a period of rejections, jaded from too much of the same thing, or uncertain about what to do next, review the options. (This list omits conventional articles, short stories, novels and non-fiction books, but it's always worth reviewing the possibility of writing in a different genre, writing 'short-short' rather than just short stories, or even writing a non-fiction book about your hobby, job, or ...)

Consider writing:

- a play – for stage, radio or TV ... or for your local school.
- a pantomime – for your local dramatic club.
- a poem – or maybe, and more 'ordinary', a verse for a greetings card.
- a 'Letter to the Editor' – of a magazine that pays for letters.
- a short story – for pre-school children.
- a children's picture-book. (A difficult market to break into – just a hundred or so words – but worth a try. YOU DON'T HAVE TO – INDEED, SHOULDN'T – DRAW THE PICTURES.)
- a picture-script for a comic-magazine character. (Many magazine characters are the copyright 'property' of the magazine publisher: freelance writers can offer story-scripts for the character, but only to the 'parent' magazine.) Again – YOU DON'T DRAW THE PIX.)
- a non-fiction picture-script – describing how something works, how to do something, or a picture-biography – probably for a children's magazine. (And again – YOU DON'T HAVE TO BE AN ARTIST.)
- a quiz – often about personality or self-improvement – requiring a choice from three possible answers to each question, on the basis of which choice, advice is offered to the participant.
- an article – '20 things you didn't know about ...' Or maybe '20 things you didn't need/want to know ...' (Note: 10 things, 12 things, 20 things all seem to 'sound' right; 7, 9, 13, 17, etc., somehow don't.)
- a filler – indeed, offer a series of short fillers on linked subjects. (It's always worth trying to sell a series of anything – a series is a 'steady earner'.)
- PR material for commercial firms. (Identify a local firm with limited publicity handouts and offer to write material for them – mail-order sales letters, brochures, hand-outs ... You know how to use words, many business people don't.)
- a puzzle – crossword, wordsearch, whatever.
- an advertising slogan – for a competition. (Competition-entering can be a full-time occupation or hobby. It requires skill with words – and a modicum of luck – but the odds are probably better than with the national lottery.)

Even if you're unsuccessful, the change'll be as good as a rest, and who knows, you might end up with a new – and lucrative – string to your bow.

12 How long is a piece of string?

Successful writers are often asked by wannabes, how long to make their story, article or book. The most helpful answer is to tell the questioner to find out for themselves, by doing some market research. But that is often less than well received. Successful writers determine these requirements by research; too many beginners expect to be handed such information on a plate.

So ... on a plate, a few very rough guidelines:

- (Paid-for) letters to editors are seldom longer than 100 words.
- Fillers can be anything from 25-word, single-sentence 'useful tips' to 200-300-word 'snippets'. (Fillers tend to be longer in American magazines.)
- General interest articles are getting shorter. They can be anything from say 400-1,500 words long, with the majority in the 800-1,000-word bracket. (A full page of a magazine, without illustrations, will be *about* 1,000 words.)
  - ◆ Longer feature articles seldom extend to more than about 2,000 words – and these will often be commissioned on an editorial idea.
- Short stories for adults are usually 1,000-2,500 words. There are some opportunities for 3,000-word stories, but 2,500 words is a more marketable length.
  - ◆ The one-page, 'coffee-break' short-short story is increasingly popular and the length has to be matched very closely to the individual magazine: these range from as short as 800 words to little more than 1,200.
  - ◆ There is virtually no market at all for the old-fashioned 10,000-word literary short story.
- Magazine serials have to be written to individual magazines' requirements but the (at least) half a dozen episodes will usually be around 4,000-5,000 words each.
- A non-fiction book will seldom be of interest if it is shorter than about 30,000 words (and that's really slim).
  - ◆ Many how-to books – such as those in this series – are around 40,000-45,000 words long.
  - ◆ More general non-fiction books – biographies, travel books, etc. – will vary widely but usually be much longer: 70,000-120,000 words perhaps.
- Novels vary considerably in their length:
  - ◆ One publisher, usually associated with magazines, currently

issuing four romance books per month in paperback on newsprint paper, specifies a 35,000-37,500 word length.

◆ Conventional present-day romances for the major paperback market however, are required to be within the 50,000-55,000-word bracket, with medical and historical romances being about 70,000 words. For other publishers, 100,000-word romances are fairly standard.

◆ Other genre novels – crime, thrillers, SF, etc. – are usually at least 80,000 words long.

◆ Current 'straight' – i.e., 'literary' – novels vary widely in length, but will seldom be shorter than 60,000-70,000 words.

◆ Blockbusters, 'sex'n'shopping', sagas, etc. are seldom shorter than 120,000 words: the sky's the limit (150,000 words is a reasonable target).

● Chapter lengths, in both fiction and non-fiction books, vary widely, but 4,000-5,000 words is a useful working average. (A thousand words is usually far too short, 10,000 is usually far too long.)

2

BASIC TECHNIQUES

- An acceptable writing style

- Studying a magazine

- Interviewing – the principles

- Interviewing – questions that get results

- The journalist's basic questions

- The title is vital

- Hooks

- Clichés

- Polishing your work

- MS presentation

- Cover sheets for articles and short stories

13 An acceptable writing style

Your writing style is a personal characteristic. In many ways, it is as individual as your signature. But magazines (and sometimes, publishers too,) often have their own style requirements. The style of writing appropriate to a tabloid newspaper varies considerably from that appropriate to an academic textbook. A writer needs to *adjust* his or her writing style to the needs of the market-place.

This checklist won't win you a Booker Prize, but it will lead to a middle-of-the-road, easy-to-read style to which few editors or publishers will object. (It is inevitably perhaps – because of my background – best suited to non-fiction writing but most of the recommendations, with a pinch of salt, are equally relevant to fiction-writing.)

● Have you read your finished piece – article, short story or book-chapter – *aloud*? Reading aloud helps you to identify the confused and/or pompous phrases in which, from time to time, we all indulge. It will also help you to identify subject/object/verb inconsistencies.

● Are all your paragraphs roughly the same length? They shouldn't be. Make some of them shorter – the occasional single-sentence paragraph often lightens up your writing. Maybe join one or two same-subject paragraphs together too – to achieve an overall variation. But aim at an *average* paragraph length of 50-80 words in articles and short stories, and up to maybe 100 words average length in books.

● How long are your sentences? If too many are over about 25 words, your writing is probably not the desirable 'easy read'. An *average* sentence length of about 15 words is a good target, but – as with paragraphs – vary the lengths widely around that average.

● Have you used too many 'difficult' words – ones whose meaning you had to check in a dictionary? (If you need to check a meaning, so too will your reader – who won't bother.) Remember, we're in the entertainment business: there's no captive market.

● Have you used many 'qualifying clauses' – such as added explanation, like this – in your writing? The whole sentence containing the explanatory clause is usually better rewritten. Keep it simple.

● Have you 'murdered your darlings'? By that, in this instance, I mean those sentences and paragraphs of which you are particularly proud; the phrases you have written so well. Rewrite them – more simply. Don't try to impress the reader with the *quality* of your writing. Just communicate.

● Does your writing still 'flow'? Shorter sentences and paragraphs, while easier to read, can lead to a rather 'bitty', jumpy style. Provide linking words and phrases between paragraphs. These links may only need to be an occasional 'and', 'but', 'also', or 'furthermore'.

● Do the first sentences in most paragraphs – particularly in articles – 'signal' the subject of the rest of the paragraph? The rest of each paragraph should expand on the opening thought. (And, of course, each paragraph should deal with only one topic; never deal with two topics in a single paragraph.)

● Have you qualified the unqualifiable? Too often one reads of

things being 'very unique'. Avoid this. And watch out for the use of clichés. If you must use a cliché, invent your own.
- Have you gone through your near-final draft and *pruned it*? Most drafts can be improved by a 10 per cent cut. The end result is 'tighter' and more readable.

Stick to the above recommendations until your sales are such that you can scrap them and develop your own writing style.

[WF]

14 Studying a magazine

You've found a magazine you'd like to contribute to; you've bought a sample issue – now you've got to study it. You need to find out what the editor wants.

First ... go out and buy another couple of issues. You can't get a good enough 'feel' of a magazine from a single issue. Then ...

- What is the overall 'tone' of the magazine? Is it brash and cheerful like a tabloid newspaper or more sedate, like a broadsheet? (Get an idea of this from the front cover and from article and story titles.)
- Who is the typical reader?
  - Is the magazine aimed at men or women only or at a general readership?
  - Look particularly at the advertisements: chair-lifts suggest older readers, spaghetti hoops and children's toys suggest mothers of primary-school kids; houses priced at £250,000 and more, and ads for French perfume suggest affluent readers, and so on. (Advertisers take pains to place ads in magazines read by those likely to use their products. Writers should use advertisers' research, in reverse.)
  - How old are the main characters in the stories? Readers identify with story characters, so teenage characters suggest teenage readers, etc.
  - Who is writing to the editor? Letters often suggest reader 'attitudes', interests, sex and age.
- Does the magazine use contributed feature articles or short stories? If not, you may be wasting your time on further study. Look at the small print on the masthead page and/or consult one of the writers' reference handbooks. (Preferably my *Magazine*

29

Writer's Handbook, biennially, from Allison & Busby.)

● What potential article subjects are covered by regular columns? There's little point in offering an article about gardening for example to a magazine with a regular gardening correspondent. (Identify regulars by their recurring by-line names.)

● Are the stories all in one genre (e.g., romance) or sometimes thrillers, or ghosties, or ...? Does the magazine favour twist-in-the-tail stories? How raunchy or inhibited are the storylines? How old are the main characters? How many characters in any one story? Whose viewpoint?

● How long are the stories and articles? Check the longest and shortest lengths of both fiction and non-fiction. (Measure column-inches per 100 mid-column words; from that, assess words per full column and complete feature or story lengths. Watch out for differing column widths – you will probably need to recount.)

● Are 'your' type of articles provided by 'ordinary' freelances or by 'names'? If you recognise the writer's name, the feature was probably commissioned – and the magazine may not be open to offers from you.

● What type of subject matter does the magazine use in its feature articles? This is a by-product of the overall 'tone': you wouldn't offer an article about improving your lover's performance in bed to a religious magazine. (You need a more subtle appreciation of the magazine's interests than that.)

● Once you've identified the type of article or story you intend to write, study the style of similar pieces in the magazine: check sentence and para lengths, long words, etc. Consider adjusting your style to suit.

[WF]

15 Interviewing – the principles

Interviews are an important tool in the armoury of a non-fiction writer. Not merely as the basis of a celebrity profile, but increasingly to get the views of 'ordinary' people, to 'flesh out' a feature article on almost any subject. Whoever the subject, an interview works best if the interviewer prepares in advance.

Some general advice on interviewing:

● Do your homework. If you are to interview a celebrity, their agent will usually be able to provide background material, biography, etc. (If not, or possibly also, consult Who's Who type books in your local library.) If you want to interview a member of the public with some special interest – an unusual illness, a survivor of an accident or disaster, or some interesting achievement – you should be able to make contact through, and get background material from, a relevant association, charity or local newspaper. Ensure you know as much as possible about your interviewee before you start an interview. If the interview is book- or film-related, read it (don't merely skim) or see it again.

- Make contact with the interviewee and arrange to meet. A visit to a celebrity's home has to be the ideal arrangement but don't reject out of hand the offer of a telephone interview.

- Prepare questions in advance. (It's better to have too many questions than too few – you don't have to use them all.) Be prepared to vary your question plan if the interview goes off on a new, *but relevant*, 'track'. (There are several standard 'ice-breaking' questions in Checklist 16. You will need interviewee-specific questions too.)

  ◆ Check, mentally, that your pre-prepared questions are appropriate – the right angle – for the magazine expected to publish the resultant feature article. Different readerships will have different interests, some more significantly than others.

  ◆ Check that your questions shouldn't cause offence.

  ◆ Check that the planned *sequence* of your questions is reasonably logical.

- Make sure you know where you are going for the interview and how to get there. Allow yourself sufficient time to arrive early ... and wait outside. Punctuality (on your part) is obligatory.

- Before leaving home/base for the interview, check that you have everything you need: notebook, pens full/pencils sharp, tape recorder (and camera if relevant) working and loaded, with spare cassettes (and/or film) and spare batteries, list of questions ready but not too obvious. If the interview is book or newspaper cutting related, take a copy with you.

- Ensure that you *look* smart, businesslike and efficient – but with 'ordinary' interviewees, not frighteningly so. It may be worth having a business card to help break the ice.

- On arrival, check that the interviewee does not object to your use of a tape recorder. If making notes too, do it quickly. Your role is to LISTEN, LISTEN, LISTEN. Before leaving, check that you have asked all necessary questions and adequately covered the ground. You seldom get a second bite at the cherry.

- An interviewee may request sight of (or possibly the right to check and approve) the finished article. Decide in advance how you will handle this request – it's up to you. Whatever you decide, promise them a copy of the published article – and keep that promise.

Note: for further advice on interviewing techniques, see *How to Write and Sell Interviews*, Sally-Jayne Wright (Allison & Busby).

16 Interviewing – questions that get results

The object of an interviewer's questions is to get an interviewee talking – revealing something about themselves.

Interview questions should be open-ended, so phrased that a yes/no response is not an option. Starting questions with one of Kipling's 'serving men' (see Checklist 17) usually helps. And make sure that you are not asking multiple questions – several in one – you'll confuse the interviewee and only get an answer to one. Or none.

Right at the start of any interview – use the interviewee's name, and be sure you get it right. Check the spelling (Ann or Anne, Jane or Jayne, etc.) and *preference* (Mike or Michael, Frederick or Fred, etc.).

There are then a number of more-or-less standard questions that will suit many interview situations – and get results. (Some have follow-ons, which can sometimes be incorporated in the main question.) Adjust these to fit:

● Tell me about your early life/childhood/family ... What did your parents do?
● Has there been a major turning point or influence in your life/career? Who or what was it?
● What, particularly, do you enjoy about your job/career?
● Tell me about the funniest/scariest/most difficult things that have happened to you in the course of your work/life/career.
● What is the greatest motivation in your life/career – a need/desire for money, power, influence, or recognition? Or what?
● If you hadn't become a writer/actress/politician/... what would you have liked to have been? Why?
● What is your greatest unfulfilled ambition? Are you making any progress?
● What is your greatest weakness? How do you cope with it?

There will, of course, be several more interviewee-specific questions. Celebrities will usually be seeking to 'sell' something – their new book or film, their business, a charity or a 'policy'. Prepare your questions about them in advance too. And get the wording right – open-ended.

17 The journalist's basic questions

> *I kept six honest serving men*
> *They taught me all I knew*
> *Their names are What and Why and When*
> *And How and Where and Who*
>
> Rudyard Kipling

Every cub journalist is/was/should be taught the things to find out when following up a 'story', or when interviewing someone. They are also the things that, as far as possible and relevant, should be incorporated in the caption for a photograph.

For the freelance non-fiction writer, they can also help to generate ideas for new articles. (See Checklist 36.) Take an everyday object and repeatedly ask yourself the basic 'Kipling' questions about it. The questions are of course fundamental to basic interviewing (see Checklist 16).

The questions? Rather than memorising Kipling's rhyme, I think of them as the five Ws and an H ... or, being of a mathematical bent, 5WH:

Who?   Who are you? Who invented/made/wrote/'dun it'? (Once you've ascertained the name, in full, and written it down, with correct spelling, always use it in subsequent conversation to ensure correctness.)

What?   What happened? What is this? What is it for? What are you/we talking about? What are/were you doing?

Why?   Why did this happen? Why did you leave/start/say that/hit him? Why were you doing/not doing that?

Where?   Where did it happen? Where are we/were you? Where are you from?

When?   When did this happen? When were you born/married/divorced/assaulted? When was this photograph taken?

How?   How did this happen? How do/did you do that? And, one of the most important questions of all ... How (Where? Who from?) can I find out more about this?

The fiction writer too will often find the above journalist's questions of use, in character formulation, in scene describing, etc. – and particularly when playing 'What if ...?'

18 The title is vital

What's the first thing you notice about a book, fiction or non-fiction? Right. The author's name or the title – whichever's biggest. What's the first thing you notice in an article or short story? Right again, the title. What's the first thing an editor notices on submitted work? Again, the title.

For book, story or article – THE TITLE IS VITAL. The purpose of a title is to seize – and hold – the attention of the passing reader.

Titles, for fiction or non-fiction, short or book-length, should be:

● Short and punchy. Life is too short to read long titles. More important, short titles are more quickly absorbed. By their nature, they are punchy. A three-word title is fine, five words should be the top limit. Short titles allow big print across the magazine page – and that's important. Short titles get noticed. Book titles have to fit the book's make-up – down the spine, on the front, and with many non-fiction books, across the top of every left-hand (*verso*) page. Too long a title won't fit in.

● Evocative – as in 'wake 'em up'. Attract the reader's attention. Evocative titles grab the fleeting eye. They stop you in your tracks. They are different – without necessarily being too different. They are instantly interesting, though. A punning article-title (see below) doesn't need to be particularly funny; a pun is effective, even if it only produces a groan.

Evocative titles for novels are rather different. You want to give some idea of what the story is about while, at the same time, titillating the prospective reader. Consult a dictionary of quotations, the Bible, or the great poets for ideas. Or maybe just use the name of your leading character.

● Informative. In the publishing world it is widely accepted that phrases like How To ..., Successful ..., Effective..., Profitable ..., in a non-fiction book's title are a great help in selling it. *How to Win Friends and Influence People* was a huge success in its day.

● Series related. If you are a novelist and envisage producing several linked stories, then series titling can help to generate both sales and the next idea. Think of Sue Grafton and her 'alphabet' mysteries – *'A' Is for Alibi*, *'B' Is for Burglar*, etc. and Susan Moody's 'Penny...' books and later, her 'bridge term' titles. Such ongoing links almost certainly also help to spark off next-book ideas.

In the non-fiction field, a publisher will often require a book title to fit into the mould of a series. Never fight such a suggestion. Books frequently sell best in series.

One way of coming up with a noticeable title – certainly for an article – is to review the various types:

- the label – an article about Chinese jade artefacts could merely be titled ... 'Jade'. (The label is usually most suited to the more 'sedate' journals.)
- the question or statement (which can be provocative) – such as 'Has he lost it?' or 'English women make the best ...'
- the quotation (or twisted quotation) – e.g., 'Lift Up Thine Eyes'.
- the exclamatory statement (or 'screamer') – as in 'Mayday!' or 'Here be Dragons!'
- the pun (even if weak) – 'The Write Approach' for example, has worked for me.

19 Hooks

Watch any newsagent or bookshop customer pondering over which magazine or book to buy. They flip magazine pages idly, they glance at the back-cover blurb of a paperback book. If something seems interesting, they stop and read the beginning. If the opening grabs them, they buy it.

As a writer, your job is to make your opening a 'grabber'. In writers' jargon, the opening is 'the hook'. It has to hook the fish.

In all types of writing, the hook needs to get the story (fact or fiction) going; explanation, fill-in, back-story can come later. The hook needs to introduce the lead character – in a personal experience article, the writer him/herself – and hint at the problem to be resolved. The hook needs to set the scene, establish the period – and the genre.

With articles or short stories you have the first 25–50 words (and the fewer the better) with which to hook the reader. With novels and non-fiction books, the first page – say 250 words maximum. (A book also needs a hook to 'bridge' between subsequent chapters.) These few words are the most important part of any article, short story, or book. Many top writers rewrite their opening para(s) again and again to get them RIGHT.

It helps to think of the types of opening there are to choose from:

For articles

- the statement of an interesting or surprising fact
- the provocative question (possibly with slight *double entendre*)
- the quotation of a recent news item on which the article 'hangs'
- the anecdote – real or invented – with dialogue

For short stories

- the ominous scene-setting
- the atmospheric description
- the historic statement
- 'active' dialogue
- the romantic meeting

For novels

- Much the same alternatives as the short story, but always including an introduction to the main character, by name, and the setting – with possibly a hint of the problem to come. Avoid use of the flashback as a hook, but some filtering in of the back-story intrigues readers and keeps them reading.

For non-fiction books

- With technical-type books of any variety, it is often useful to start by listing what is to be dealt with within the book and/or the chapter – possibly with a bullet-pointed list.
- 'Storyline' non-fiction books are best treated like novels – introduce subject (character or event, etc.), time, and setting straight away.

20 Clichés

It was film magnate Sam Goldwyn who advised that clichés should be avoided like the plague. His advice is equally appropriate to writers.

Best-selling author Iris Gower was *slightly* kinder; she advised wannabe writers, 'If you must use a cliché – make up one of your own.'

In everyday life though, most of us sprinkle our speech generously with clichés; in fictional dialogue they are therefore acceptable – even A Good Thing. But only in dialogue, which it makes realistic, not in descriptive passages, etc.

In non-fiction writing, clichés should be avoided – but they have a tendency to slip in unnoticed. Done-to-death clichés to watch out for include:

> The writing's on the wall
> Like the plague
> Back to square one
> At this moment in time
> As quick as a flash
> Jobs for the boys
> Blissful ignorance
> Takes the biscuit
> Alive and well and living in
> Live now, pay later
> Chickens coming home to roost
> Doctor in the house
> The fair(er) sex
> The good news ... the bad news
> Coals to Newcastle
> A hive of industry

Not only are clichés often a sign of lazy writing – they have a tendency to generalise and approximate – but they can so easily make writing out-dated. To quote an extreme, 'Can I do you now, sir?' was a catch-phrase from a 1940s comedy show; in those days it soon became a cliché, today it means little to anyone other than OAPs.

BUT ... H. W. Fowler, in his *Modern English Usage,* points out that not all uses of clichés are to be deprecated. 'Writers would be need-lessly handicapped if they were never allowed to say that something was a *foregone conclusion*, ... or that someone was *feathering his nest* or ... had *a bee in his bonnet.*' They are readily recognisable – and useful – phrases which present themselves for deliberate adoption or rejection.

21 Polishing your work

Too many novice writers think that, once they have finished writing their article, story or book, that's it. They leave undone the essential polishing. The first draft of an article, story or book is fine – but the work is not yet ready for submission. Inevitably, there will be lots of little things (and some big ones too) wrong with it. Some writers work their way through several drafts of their work before submitting it.

Apply the process outlined below. The more often you work through it, the less productive it will become – and there is a school of thought that recommends only limited polishing, to preserve the original spontaneity. But some polishing is ALWAYS necessary. It's up to you to strike the right balance.

● First, count the words. If your first draft (article, story or book chapter) is too long, that's fine: you can cut it (see below). If overall, it's too short, the problem is more difficult: you've got to put more into it – which may entail doing more research or adding another twist to the plot.

● Next, check paragraph and sentence lengths (see Writing Style, Checklist 13), and maybe the proportion of dialogue to narrative in your fiction. If any of these differ too much from the publishers' or magazine's usual style, it will probably be wise to amend them. Reducing paragraph lengths is easy – just break them in two. To shorten over-long sentences, replace the mid-sentence AND – there are always some – with a full stop. As long as the dialogue still moves the story forward, you can perhaps increase it by talking about the situation rather than describing it in narrative. (cf., Show – don't tell, Checklist 57)

● Read through and delete everything that is superfluous, anything the piece can do without – 'tighten it up'.
  ◆ This can be a simple deletion of 'excess' adjectives or 'just noticed' repetitive statements and tautologies.
  ◆ Check for irrelevant phrases and sentences.
  ◆ Watch out particularly for qualification of the unqualifiable: *very unique* is a common mistake – comparable with being *slightly pregnant*.
  ◆ Where the same word has been used closely adjacent to another, think of an alternative.
  ◆ Watch out for 'preaching' passages: if you want to preach, get a soapbox or pulpit.

- Read the piece aloud. This will help you to identify the pompous phrases and expressions that we all use occasionally. Delete or replace them. Reading aloud will also identify those sections of which you are particularly proud – the 'well-turned phrase', the imaginatively descriptive but overlong word – these too are often pompous and should be rewritten, more simply.

- Having tightened up your writing and adjusted your sentences and paragraphs, check that the writing still *flows*. It may be a good idea to re-link the paragraphs – one simple method is to add in an 'And' or a 'But' at the start of a following para.

- Check that the whole story or article is CLEAR. Put it aside for a while – as long as possible, within reason – and come back to it fresh, as a 'new reader'.

- Check your facts. If you're not absolutely sure, or if two reference books disagree, there's a lot to be said for hedging your bets: 'It is said ...' or 'About ...'

- Check your punctuation:

  ◆ I'm prone to overuse of the dash – the lazy person's punctuation mark. Sometimes, I go back over my work and get rid of some of the dashes but usually not, because it goes with the casual writing style that I prefer. (Anyway, that's my story and I'm sticking to it.)

  ◆ As far as possible, avoid using an exclamation mark in other than dialogue: it's usually the hallmark of an incompetent writer who cannot convey excitement/emotion through the words alone.

  ◆ Check your commas – be sparing in their use.

  ◆ If you have used colons and semicolons, check that you've used them correctly. (It's often better/easier to avoid using them.)

- Finally, count the words again. Confirm that the piece is now/still the required length – or do something about it. And read it all through again to confirm that with all your amendments it still makes overall sense.

Remember though: too much polishing can be counter-productive. It can knock the stuffing out of your writing, deflate your enthusiasm and make it all bland and dull. Take care of that balance – but you must do SOME polishing.

22 MS presentation

- Your work must be typed, – any *conventional* typeface and with a newish typewriter/printer ribbon – in double-spacing, on one side only of white A4 paper
- Allow good wide margins on all sides: something like 1.5 inches left, 1.0 inch right, top and bottom – and more is better. (Most editors prefer the typescript to have ragged right-hand line-ends – i.e., not 'justified'.)
- It must be typed on 'reasonable' paper. Not too thin – but not too thick either, or the postage will be excessive. Best use 80 gsm (grammes per square metre) paper. If using fan-fold paper in a computer printer, always strip off the hole-punched edges and separate the sheets.
- The pages must be numbered. Provide an identification 'strap' – i.e., a header – too, such as 'Title/surname/page number' in top right corner.
- Mark the end of the article or story with a row of dots and the word END (in caps). At the end of the last page also give your (pen- and real) name and address. Use a phrase such as 'Bill Bloggs (writing as Belinda Bloggson).'
- Provide a cover sheet to the article or story. (For details of cover sheets, see Checklist 23.)
- Also provide a BRIEF covering letter. It should be little more than something like, 'I enclose a 000-word article, TITLE, for your consideration for publication at your usual rates of payment. If not of interest, please return.' Don't mention the coffee-stain on page 3 – retype it; don't ask after the editor's health – he/she might tell you.
- Manuscript, covering letter and SAE should all pack neatly into a new, not recycled envelope. If not, use a bigger one. (A 1,500-word typescript plus covering letter, etc. can usually be folded twice and sent in a DL-sized envelope. Anything longer needs a C5 or larger envelope.) Some writers don't even fold short manuscripts.
- Always enclose a stamped addressed envelope. Make sure it is big enough, and adequately stamped, to accommodate the bouncing typescript. If you don't send an SAE, your work could well go directly to the WPB – unconsidered.
- KEEP A COPY.

[WF]

40

23 Cover sheets for articles and short stories

It is always a good idea to provide a cover sheet for your articles and short stories. First, it helps to make the submission *look good* (and good presentation is half the battle). Secondly, editors supposedly scribble the payment due on the cover sheet and pass it to the accounts section, retaining the manuscript for editing. That way you should get paid quicker – which is worth encouraging.

American writing books often specify title positions, etc., with precise measurements: in Britain, just put them in roughly the right place; UK editors are not so fussy. One way of setting out a cover sheet is as follows.

For all cover sheets:

- Set page margins at about 1.5 inches left, 1.0 inch top, bottom and right.
- About half-way down the A4 page, centrally on the line, in capitals, *not* underlined, the title. (This, and the by-line below can, if wished, be in bold – but only these two lines.) If there is a subtitle, down two (single-spaced) lines and type it, in lower case, not underlined.
- Down four (single-spaced) lines, centrally on the line, in lower case, not underlined, your name, or pen-name if to be used.
- About ten (single-spaced) lines further down, starting at the left margin, type something like, 'Approximately 000 words on 00 sheets of typescript.' (For under, say, 800-word pieces, give the word count to the nearest fifty words; 800-plus, to the nearest hundred. Never the supposedly exact figure from your word processor.)
- If the submission is an illustrated article, I follow the word count statement with, '... accompanied by 00 black-and-white photographs, by the writer, plus a caption sheet.' (Stating that pix are by the writer saves the magazine having to check this with you. If illustrations are by anyone else you should give details, name and address, etc., for separate payment.)
- Near the foot of the page (allowing enough room to accommodate all), starting at left margin, type your (real) name (if using a pen-name, add 'writing as Belinda Bloggson') and address as it would be (single-spaced) on an envelope.
- Finally, beneath, your phone and fax numbers. (If relevant, your e-mail address too.)

- I give all my articles and stories a reference number and file name. I include this on my cover sheets too – last line, hard against the right margin.

For fiction only:

- For stories, it is important to make clear which rights are being offered. So ... in top right corner of the sheet, type 'FBSR offered' (or 'First British – or whatever – Serial Rights offered'.)

  (With articles, this is seldom necessary: in Britain, the offer of First British Serial Rights is always assumed. If offering work to America though, it may be worth specifying the rights offered. For fiction, other rights can easily be on offer.)

3
ESSENTIAL EQUIPMENT AND WORKING PRACTICES

- A writer's equipment

- Get the most from your word processor

- Essential reference books

- Often overlooked research sources

- More effective research

- Coping with writers' block

- How to get help

- Check your telephone technique

- Criticism – giving and taking

- Writing organisations

- Useful names and addresses for writers

- Books worth reading – just for 'inspiration'

24 A writer's equipment

It doesn't take much in the way of equipment to set up as a writer. But the days are long gone when all that was needed was pen and paper, plus bum on seat. Forget tales of writing in pencil in school exercise books or submitting handwritten work on the back of old computer print-out. At the turn of the millennium, a writer NEEDS a certain minimum amount of equipment:

43

- At the absolute minimum, a typewriter; far better, a word processor. Most writers just cannot afford to pay for someone else to type their handwritten work for them. And typing your own work is an excellent opportunity for doing some of the polishing – see Checklist 21.
- A good stock of paper – white, A4 (unlined, of course), ideally 80 gsm.
- A stock of white DL-sized 'business' envelopes (11 x 22 cm) for correspondence and articles or stories of not more than about 1,500 words. (It is cheapest to buy DL envelopes in boxes of 1,000 – they'll soon go.) You'll also need a smaller supply of C4 and C5 manila envelopes for longer pieces.
- You need to keep copies of everything you write – articles, stories, correspondence, etc. – so, a supply of lever-arch and ordinary cardboard files. I keep copies of articles, day-to-day correspondence, etc., in lever-arch files and finished book manuscripts in ordinary 'flat' files.
- Pens, pencils, rubbers, sticky tape, 'white-out' correction liquid (it isn't ALWAYS necessary to reprint a word-processed page with just a tiny error), paper-clips, stapler and staples ('Bambi' size is ideal – and cheap), spare typewriter ribbons or printer cartridges, and blank computer disks (for own back-up and, increasingly, to meet editorial requirements).
- An account book – I use one with 14 cash columns (see Checklist 95).
- Worth its weight in gold (saving 'weighing trips' to the post office) but hardly an early necessity, a really *accurate* postage scale.
- Later, when affordable, a filing cabinet will be a good investment.
- Even later, when you KNOW you need them: 'dedicated' phone, answering machine, fax machine and, probably, modem and Internet connection.

25 Get the most from your word processor

These days, most writers use a word processor. They're no longer impossibly expensive and should no longer be frightening. Their advantages are legion. Not every writer though, makes the most use of their computer: they set them up (or get a friend to set 'em up) for writing and fail to explore their full facilities. These suggestions may help you to get more out of your word processor. They're by no means comprehensive – I seem to find a new 'wrinkle' every few days – and may need to be done slightly differently on your program. (Nowadays, I use Word 97™ and all the hints are based on using that program.)

- Design yourself a letterhead – avoid 'fancy' fonts (stick to one or two plain ones in the heading) and OTT 'clip art' and keep it simple – include an automatically updated date *field*, and then save it as a document. Every time you want to write a letter, open the file and start writing. (I find an ordinary file more convenient than a *template*.)
- Don't save all your writing work in just one big directory or folder – open sub-folders and sub-sub-folders. Organise your filing in a tree-like system. (Windows 95 and Word 97 come with a 'My Documents' folder. Within that I have sub-folders for Articles, Books, Courses, Money, etc. I open sub-sub-folders within the Books folder for each book that I write.
- As you do more writing and save each document on your hard disk, the list of files gets longer and longer. And if you take advantage of the long file names now permissible (in Windows 95) the file list becomes increasingly hard to manage. Restrict your file names to the 'old-fashioned' eight characters – develop a system. (I call each book by a three- or four-character 'set' and follow that with 'C' (for chapter) and then a number, starting with 01 or NTRO (for Intro). Thus, everything written for this book is 99ck and chapter one is 99ckc01; if there were to be illustrations, they would be filed as 99ckc01a, b, etc.
- Explore your word processor's opportunities for using keyboard shortcuts. These are often quicker to use than the mouse. For example, I can centre a heading merely by keying Ctrl+E and embolden it by Ctrl+B; this is much quicker than taking my hands off the keyboard and moving the mouse up to the menus at the top of the screen.
- If your program, like Word 97, offers toolbars at the screen edge, containing buttons for specific actions, you can probably personalise these. I have an extra toolbar containing the buttons I most use – font and font-size, header, word count, print envelope, ruler on/off and 'Save to', for instance. I switch off most other toolbars (and the ruler) unless I need them for a particular task. My screen is less cluttered. (Since customising that toolbar, I have discovered that I can activate the 'Save to' command more quickly merely by keying F12, another keyboard shortcut.)

- Don't forget, also, the commands that can be accessed by *right*-clicking on your mouse. And you can customise this right-click menu, too. There are often three or four ways of *skinning the cat* – toolbar button, keyboard shortcut, right-click menus or the standard drop-down menus. Use whichever shortcut is most appropriate from where you are at any particular time.

- If your wp program has 'Auto-correct' and/or 'Auto-text' facilities you can use these for a whole lot of time-saving things:

  - When I type my initials followed by L, the auto-correct facility immediately replaces that with my name and (slightly abbreviated) address spread out in a single line (for article-ends).

  - I am prone to misspell the word *relate* (among many others) – my fingers move too fast for my own good – but now, all the likely wrong spellings are instantly corrected by the machine. Similarly with *and* and *to*, among others.

  - I occasionally need symbols when preparing small posters or brochures. Keying in TX produces a drawing of a telephone; keying in FX gets me a drawing of a computer disk.

  - When preparing an index recently, I needed to repeat the same (short) string of page numbers in many items. I arranged for a set of letters to be replaced instantly by the needed string of page numbers.

  - My initials plus AD followed by F3 instantly generates my name, address and tel/fax number in a neat five-line block (for article cover sheets).

  - I write to different individuals within my publishers' office. The firm's name and address immediately replaces ABX followed by F3; individual names are instantly corrected from their initials.

One problem with these 'instant replacements' is that you have to ensure the non-use of the abbreviations for any other purpose. (I once arranged for M1, M2, M3, etc to be my 'shorthand' for January, February, March, etc. This was fine until I started typing motorway travel directions ...) Adding an X to a troublesome abbreviation usually solves the problem. You also need to ensure that the program will work from both lower case and capital letters.

All these, or similar, facilities are readily available on most of today's word processors – it's just a matter of identifying what can be done and what will be most useful to you. Make your writing life easier whenever you can.

[WM]

26 Essential reference books

Within their own specialised field every writer, whether of fiction or non-fiction, will have collected together the necessary reference books. And of course, these will vary with the specialism. As well as the specialist reference books though, every writer needs the books relevant to the *whole* craft of writing. The books listed below, all of which are on my own shelves, will provide a firm foundation upon which you can build your own library.

- A good (thick) dictionary – my own is the *Concise Oxford Dictionary* but I also frequently consult my wife's much bigger Longman's *Dictionary of the English Language*. No matter how good, the computer's spell-check doesn't afford so much help. (I also often consult the smaller *Little Oxford Dictionary* – it's less of a handful.)
- A thesaurus – my own is the Penguin *Roget* but I also find myself referring to the easier-to-use tiny Collins Gem Thesaurus.
- A writers' dictionary   mine is *The Oxford Writers' Dictionary* (paperback). Invaluable for sorting out when/whether to use *ise* or *ize*, 'what on earth do those initials stand for' – and should you use full stops between the letters, when to use italics and when not, and similar 'problems'. I also still refer, from time to time, to the earlier *Oxford Dictionary for Writers and Editors* (OUP).
- Somewhat overtaken by the above, I still find *Hart's Rules for Compositors and Readers* (OUP) useful.
- A compact encyclopaedia – my favourite of the several I've got is the five-volume paperback *Wordsworth Encyclopaedia*. (It only cost £10 and is worth its weight...) Other first-reference favourites are the single-volume Macmillan and Penguin Encyclopaedias.
- Fowler's *Modern English Usage* as revised by Sir Ernest Gowers (OUP). Not simply a reference book, it's great for browsing too. So too, is Gower's *Complete Plain Words* (HMSO).
- Dictionaries of quotations (I can't resist them) – of the several on my shelves, the most 'reliable', and well-thumbed is the *Everyman Dictionary of Quotations and Proverbs*, compiled by D. C. Browning (Dent) with the more modern, differently organised *Chronological Dictionary of Quotations*, edited by Edmund Wright (Bloomsbury) coming a close second. I also constantly refer to *Writers on Writing*, compiled by Jon Winokur (Headline) – I enjoy dipping into that at random, just for the hell of it.

- *The Chronicle of the 20th Century* (Dorling Kindersley); *Encyclopaedia of Dates and Events*, Pascoe, Lee and Jenkins (Teach Yourself Books – EUP); *Chronology of the Modern World 1763–1965*, Neville Williams (Penguin). These three books are complementary – and really useful to all writers.
- The writers' market reference books: choose between the oldest inhabitant, the *Writers' & Artists' Yearbook* and the yellow-covered *Writer's Handbook*, and/or my own biennial *Magazine Writer's Handbook* (which deals with far fewer markets in far more detail). In all cases, it's really important to have the latest issue – all three go out of date quickly.

27 Often overlooked research sources

Research always sounds like hard work – until you get started, and then it's often fun. Many writers equate research with much studying of 'primary' sources, entailing head-grinding study in dusty library and museum archives. This may be essential if you are writing a definitive non-fiction book –a biography or history – but is seldom necessary for most fiction and many general-interest feature articles.

Before you dig too deep, consider these often overlooked research sources. They may be all you need.

- Ask the man or woman who knows. Many writers overlook asking the obvious person for help. Most people will be happy to help with information about their hobby, sport, interest or job (as long as you're no threat to their livelihood).
- Don't be embarrassed. Consult children's reference books first. Simple facts may be all you need – and nowhere are they so simply explained as in children's books, such as those from Ladybird, Funfax, Usborne or Dorling Kindersley.
- As well as second-hand bookshops, investigate the 'Bargain Books' bookshops, or the bargain display counters in large 'ordinary' bookshops. Bargain books are sold off cheap by publishers, because of declining sales and shortage of warehouse storage space – or because they are only of specialist interest. If your need coincides with that specialism, you get a real bargain. Ask the excellent Bibliophile Books, of 5 Thomas Road, London E14 7BN (Tel: 0171-515 9222) to put you on the mailing list for their regular catalogues of bargain books.

- Don't overlook relevant magazine and newspaper articles. Tear them out or photocopy them. They can help to update older book sources.
- Collect informative 'giveaway' brochures and the like. A free brochure from the Dieppe Tourist Office provided all that I needed for a story about a school day trip.
- Watch out for informative series of advertisements and such things as beer mats with interesting snippets on their reverse. Collect them and file them away carefully.
- Collect books of interesting and unusual facts – the 'Would You Believe It' sort. They're always helpful.
- Look out for interesting books on your visits to country houses, etc. They may not be (so readily) available elsewhere. Also old catalogues, posters, etc.
- If you need information about one special, not-too-long-ago day, you can often buy that day's newspapers. Consult the small ads in the 'quality' Sunday newspapers – they are usually offered as 'for your birth date'.
- Check Open University and/or BBC 'Learning Zone' TV and radio programmes. If there is anything on 'your' subject, you're well away. And of course, all the other marvellous factual TV programmes.

[WF]

For more on researching, relevant to both fiction and general, non-specialist non-fiction, see Jean Saunders' *How to Research Your Novel* (Allison & Busby).

28 More effective research

Research is not a one-off exercise – nor can it be thought of as something that comes naturally to all writers. Most of us can improve our research activities.

These suggestions may help:

- As you collect material ... FILE IT. A shoe-box full of unrelated cuttings is of little use. The same cuttings separated by subject, filed in identifiable recycled envelopes, or if you're affluent, clear plastic envelopes, can be a long-lasting gold-mine. Stick related small cuttings onto A4 sheets.
- Similarly, make notes from borrowed books, etc. on A4 sheets and file by subject. For later check-referencing, note the book page

number of important items. Make a note too of the book's ISBN and from where it was borrowed.

- Cross-check your research – if necessary go back to primary sources, but this is not always possible. Always try to check one secondary source against another though. If the 'facts' DON'T check out, and you can't leave it out, then qualify your statement – say something like 'It seems likely that...'

- Make sure your research is as up to date as possible – and if writing a book, remember that there are often lengthy delays between writing the manuscript and completing copy-editing and receiving page proofs. With variable information – current prices, names, etc. – check and correct just before manuscript delivery, before typesetting and again, if possible, at page proof. (Beware though, making layout-affecting changes at proof stage.)

- Never overlook your local library – and particularly the children's section. Your friendly librarian will usually be only too glad to help with something other than finding someone the next family saga in large print.

- Never be afraid of asking anyone, no matter how famous, for information. Explain why you want it and you'll usually be successful. The worst that can happen is for them to say no. (I believe in making first contact by letter, rather than phoning 'cold'.)

- When you contact a research source and have extracted all they have to offer, always ask for suggestions of other people who might be able to help – seek to build chains of contact-informants. (And note the areas of expertise, names, addresses, etc. of all your contacts for future use. Develop an alphabetical list by information-area.)

- If a research-contact gives you oral permission to reproduce a picture or use a quotation, confirm this permission in writing and file the correspondence – you may need it later.

29 Coping with writers' block

Every now and then most writers – particularly of fiction – come to a grinding halt. They can't think what to write next, or how to write it; their imagination seems to have gone sour on them – a 'will I ever write again' panic sets in. This is a condition known as writers' block. (It seldom happens to non-fiction writers, who are usually working from a detailed synopsis.) Different writers have different ways of coping with the problem, including some of the following:

- First, a bit 'heavy', but it's worth getting it out of the way. Check that there is not some outside influence causing the *block* – the overdraft, the children, a virus, lack of sleep, a hangover. Do whatever you can to alleviate any such non-writing problem – concentrate on solving that before you try to write again. (For many, their writing is often a way of relieving the outside stress.)
- Check your writing environment – relative chair and keyboard height, back support, monitor height and screen angle, lighting on notes, glare on screen etc. Can you make any improvements?
- Stop worrying about the *block*. You WILL get over it. The initial worry generates its own further stress in a continuing spiral of depression. Think about something totally different for a while.
- Get yourself a quick cup of tea or coffee – or better perhaps, a large slug of something strong and alcoholic. (It may not be an instant cure for the *block* but it should make you feel better about it ... for now.)
- Walk – or even bath – the dog/cat/...
- Go back one or two pages within your manuscript ... retype it, revising as you go, hopefully getting back into the swing of it.
- Share your problem with a writer friend – someone who will UNDERSTAND.
- Write a chatty letter to a friend – or even to the bank manager – on a totally different matter.
- Play 'What if ...?'
- Indulge yourself – pamper yourself with a hot bath, a meal out, an afternoon's television or a trip to the cinema/theatre ... even put the diet on hold and pig out on a box of chocolates.
- Make a list of alternative scenarios to get you out of the 'fictional black hole' which is your *block*. Be as ridiculous, as fantastic, as improbable as you like in developing this list: then sit down and brainstorm about the alternatives – maybe one of them is not as impossible as you thought.
- Write anything – 'force' yourself, even if it's not obviously 'getting anywhere', even if it's abject rubbish – for, say, ten minutes.

30 How to get help

We all need help, in some form or another, from time to time from others. You should never be afraid of asking for help: after all, the person you're approaching can always say no. And next time, who knows, it may be them seeking your help. On the whole most people, and particularly writers, are pretty helpful to one another – as long as helping doesn't take TOO-OO-OO long. A few guidelines:

- A quick, 'to-the-point' phone call is often the best approach and is easiest to respond to. After initial pleasantries though, always check that it is a convenient moment for your contact to spare the time. Offer to phone back later.
- Differentiate between 'What's the name of the editor at ...?' or 'How do I write *Yes, darling* in Swedish?' questions and those where you're asking for something written, that you can quote. For the latter, a written request (with a SAE) is probably more appropriate.
- If you don't get a reply to a written query you must decide whether to chase it up – and risk a brush-off – or forget it. Are you in too much of a hurry?
- If you are seeking research-type information, most people are surprisingly happy to help, pleased that you have thought of them. It's also always worth asking if your contact knows of anyone else who might have relevant information – develop a chain of contacts.
- If you are seeking a lot of information, offer to meet over a drink or meal (at your expense). Is this likely to be value for money?
- If you need an agreement vetting, or have any problem with a publisher the Society of Authors (see Checklist 33) will always help members – and if you've reached that stage, it's time you joined.
- If, as a novice writer, you are seeking general advice on how to write, the best source of such help is often your local writers' circle – or try one of the several weekend or longer conferences. Most successful writers remember what it was like when they were starting out and are very approachable – just don't monopolise them.

31 Check your telephone technique

The telephone is part of our everyday working lives. It's marvellous; we couldn't do without it. That's when we're initiating the calls. But when we ourselves are interrupted by the phone, it's a bloomin' nuisance. (And yes, I know it's not hard to block calls, or filter them through the answering machine, but sometimes...)

Whenever you phone someone, for information or whatever, always remember that you are interrupting them – breaking into their chain of thought.

Keep these points in mind:

- Don't phone unless it's really important – to you or to the person you're calling.
- Always have a note-pad and pen/pencil handy – your memory is NOT infallible.
- Before you pick up the phone, decide broadly what you're going to say or ask – list the points you want to clarify or put across. Again, don't rely on your memory – you're bound to forget something.
- Once you've got through, check that you've reached the person you want – and if it's a first-time contact, make a note of their name, and use it during the ensuing conversation.
- Give your own name to the person you're calling– and don't say it too fast. (Use first name and last name – NEVER call yourself Mr or Mrs.) Your voice is not instantly recognisable – even to friends.
- Say why you are calling – identify the subject. Remember that, while the subject is uppermost in your mind, it is unlikely to be so in the mind of the person you're calling.
- Throughout the conversation, be polite, businesslike, and straight-forward. Be as brief as possible – but not abrupt or curt. Don't chat – unless the person you are calling invites you to.
- Smile while you're talking – 'smile as you dial' – you will sound friendly; stand up while you're talking if you want to sound posi-tive/assertive. Believe me, it works.
- All the while you are talking, make notes of what you are told, or have agreed. Don't wait until after you put the phone down.
- At the end of the phone call, read back your notes to the person at the other end to make sure that you have correctly heard/inter-preted what has been said and agreed.
- If the content of the phone discussion was particularly important (to you), it's often worth confirming the result in a BRIEF letter – 'for the record'.
- If you're on the receiving end of a call, make a note of the caller's name – and use it during conversation to ensure you've got it right.

Work to those 'rules' and your telephone technique will surely improve.

32 Criticism – giving and taking

The basis of many writers' groups – circles, evening classes, work-shops, etc. – is the oral criticism of written work by the group as a whole, or by the tutor or workshop leader. Such *critiques* (a ghastly word imported from America, even worse when used as the verb *to critique*) are inevitably like the curate's egg. Some are helpful and constructive, some are worthless and destructive, some have good points worth noting – but worthwhile advice is often hidden amongst a plethora of time-wasting nit-picks.

A major criticism of the whole practice is that we are all writing mainly for silent reading, not for reading aloud, which is a discipline in which many writers are unpractised and unskilled. The other major objection to the whole process is that each critic has to listen atten-tively (always difficult) and react instantly (even harder) – which can lead to an airing of prejudices.

(Some groups offer the opportunity for a quick read – at least by the tutor/leader – of others' work before the criticism session. This is obviously an improvement, but is not always practical.)

Nevertheless, 'instant' round-circle or tutor crits are a feature of the writing world; it behoves us all to learn to give – and take – them.

When criticising:

● Listen carefully, concentrate on the words, not the presentation.
● Try to find something complimentary to say about the work – before being critical.
● Watch for significant faults rather than nit-picks. (An uninten-tional change of viewpoint is more important than a single word used wrongly or an indulgence of commas.)
● While avoiding over-playing your own prejudices, it is worth concentrating on watching out for a few specific types of fault – cardboard characters, stilted dialogue, viewpoint changes, etc. (You could even compliment the writer on not having the faults you were watching for.)
● Where possible, be tentative in your criticism – 'You might like to have a look at …'

When being criticised:

● Listen carefully and politely – even the daftest, most worthless crit may contain one or two nuggets. Make notes of all the comments – you can sort them out afterwards.

● Try not to take the crit too personally – it's your work that's being torn to shreds, not you. And remember: in the end, you make your own judgement.

● Consider who is doing the criticising – pretentious wannabe or experienced pro. Is their advice likely to be soundly based? But remember the 'nuggets in the mire' point, above.

● Don't REACT. Thank your critics politely and promise to consider their comments.

When your published work is criticised:

● Remember that you got it published – you 'won'. Follow-up argument is almost always petty and demeaning.

● Don't respond to a critical published review; don't answer back. (Some reviewers believe it's their duty to find fault.) But if there is a factual mistake in the review, write – calmly and politely – to the publication to correct it.

33 Writing organisations

There are a number of writers' organisations in Britain, ranging from professional associations through specialist groups to conferences and writers' circles. It pays us all to belong to a professional/trade association; most people can benefit from membership of a relevant specialist group... and getting together with those of like mind, at conferences, etc., helps to keep us sane.

Writers' circles vary: good ones, geared to publication, can be an enormous help to anyone; tea-party-based mutual admiration societies being 'creative' can be the death of any wannabe's professional writing career.

Contact details for various organisations are given below – but these details sometimes become out-dated, so address correspondence to the official title, marking envelopes 'Please forward', thereby saving redirection postage.

Professional/trade associations

● The National Union of Journalists, Acorn House, 314 Gray's Inn Road, London WC1X 8DP. Tel: 0171-278 7916.

- The Society of Authors, 84 Drayton Gardens, London SW10 9SB. Tel: 0171-373 6642.
- The Writers' Guild of Great Britain, 430 Edgware Road, London W2 1EH. Tel: 0171-723 8074.

Major specialist groups

- The Author-Publisher Network, Chairman, Clive Brown, 26 Ladymeade, Ilminster, Somerset TA19 0EA.
- The Crime Writers' Association, Secretary, Judith. Cutler, 60 Drayton Road, Kings Heath, Birmingham B14 7LR.
- The Romantic Novelists' Association, Chairman, Angela Arney, 43 Wilton Gardens, Shirley, Southampton SO1 2QS.
- The Society of Women Writers and Journalists, Secretary, Jean Hawkes, 110 Whitehall Road, Chingford, London E4 6DW.
- The Women Writers Network, contact Susan Kerr, 55 Burlington Lane, London W4 3ET.

... and various sub-groups – technical, children's, medical, etc. – within, and only for members of, the Society of Authors.

Selected major annual conferences

- Annual Writers' Conference (at Winchester, previously at Southampton University), a June weekend annually. Organiser, Barbara Large, 'Chinook', Southdown Road, Winchester, Hants SO21 2BY. Tel: 01962-712307.
- Scottish Association of Writers Weekend School, annually, in March. Contact Sheila Livingstone, 36 Cloan Crescent, Bishop-briggs, Glasgow G64 2HL.
- The Southern Writers' Conference, a June weekend annually, at Earnley, near Chichester. Secretary, Lucia White, Stable House, Home Farm, Coldharbour Lane, Dorking, Surrey RH4 3JG. Tel: 01306-876202.
- The Writers' Holiday (at Caerleon) annually, in July. Contact D.L. Anne Hobbs, 30 Pant Road, Newport NP9 5PR. Tel: 01633-854976
- The Writers' Summer School ('Swanwick') annually, in August. Secretary, Brenda Courtie, The Rectory, Blisworth, Northants NN7 3BJ. Tel: 07050-630949

Writers' circles

These are to be found all over the country. Enquire at your local library for your nearest circle. Or write to Jill Dick, 'Oldacre', Horderns Park Road, Chapel-en-le-Frith, Derbyshire SK12 6SY enclosing a blank cheque marked 'Not exceeding £5' for the latest edition (including postage) of her comprehensive *Directory of Writers' Circles.*

34 Useful names and addresses for writers

Arvon Foundation, The, Kilnhurst, Kilnhurst Road, Todmorden, Lancs OL14 6AX. Tel: 01706 816582. Fax: 01706 816359.
Authors' Agents, The Association of, 37 Goldhawk Road, London W12 8QQ. Tel: 0181-749 0315. Fax: 0181-749 0318.
Authors' Licensing and Collecting Society Ltd (ALCS), Marlborough Court, 14-18 Holborn, London EC1N 2LE. Tel: 0171-395 0600. Fax: 0171-395 0660.
Author-Publisher Network, The, 26 Ladymeade, Ilminster, Somerset TA19 0EA.
Authors, The Society of, 83 Drayton Gardens, London SW10 9SB. Tel: 0171-373 6642.
Book Trust, The, Book House, 45 East Hill, London SW18 2QZ. Tel: 0181-870 9055.
BBC Broadcast (Radio), Broadcasting House, London W1A 1AA. Tel: 0171-580 4468.
BBC Broadcast (TV), Television Centre, Wood Lane, London W12 7RJ. Tel: 0181-743 8000.
British Library, The, 96 Euston Road, London NW1 2DB. Tel: 0171-412 7111. Fax: 0171-412 7268.
British Library Newspaper Library, Colindale Avenue, London NW9 5HE. Tel: 0171-412 7353. Fax: 0171-412 7379.
Comic Creators Guild, c/o 20b Mountgrove Road, London N5 2LS. Tel: 0181-699 0218.
Contributions Agency, The, (DSS) Newcastle-upon-Tyne NE98 1YX. Tel: 0191-213 5000.
Copyright Licensing Agency Ltd., 90 Tottenham Court Road, London W1P 0LP. Tel: 0171-436 5931. Fax: 0171-436 3986.
Greeting Card Association, The, 41 Links Drive, Elstree WD6 3PP. Tel/fax: 0181-236 0024.
Indexers, Society of, Mermaid House, 1 Mermaid Court, London SE1 1HR. Tel: 0171-403 4947.

New Science Fiction Alliance (NSFA), c/o BBR, PO Box 625, Sheffield S1 3GY.

PEN International (English Centre), 7 Dilke Street, London SW3 4JE. Tel: 0171-352 6303. Fax: 0171-351 0220.

PA News Library, The, 292 Vauxhall Bridge Road, London SW1V 1AE. Tel: (Direct line – News Librarian) 0171-963 7015. Fax: 0171-963 7065.

PLR (Public Lending Right) Office, The Registrar, Bayheath House, Prince Regent Street, Stockton-on-Tees TS18 1DF. Tel:01642 604699. Fax: 01642 615641.

St. James Awards, The Ian, The New Writers' Club, PO Box 60, Cranbrook, Kent TN17 2ZR. Tel: 01580 212626.

Women Writers and Journalists, The Society of, 110 Whitehall Road, London E4 6DW. Tel:0181-529 0886.

Women Writers Network, 55 Burlington Lane, London W4 3ET. Tel: 0181-994 0598.

Writers' Guild of Great Britain, The, 430 Edgware Road, London W2 1EH. Tel: 0171-723 8074. Fax: 0171-706 2413.

35 Books worth reading – just for 'inspiration'

Every writer who has been at the game for any length of time collects books about writing: reference books, how-to books – and books which inspire, that 'ring a bell', that have helped them along the way. These are some of my inspirations; I think you will find that they are at least worth a look.

- *Performing Flea – A Self-Portrait in Letters*, P. G. Wodehouse. My copy of this is as one of three autobiographical books published in one volume by Penguin as *Wodehouse on Wodehouse*, 1981. The book is a collection of letters – mostly advice and criticism about writing – written over the period from the 1920s to the 1950s, to his friend, and initially struggling writer, Bill Townsend. Not only are they full of advice to all writers but also amusing and witty.

- *Waterhouse on Newspaper Style*, Keith Waterhouse, (Viking). In the late 1970s Keith Waterhouse, at that time writing regularly for the *Daily Mirror*, was asked to set down his thoughts about the use of language in the popular press. The result, *Daily Mirror Style*, was privately published for the *Daily Mirror* in late 1979. (It was/is not a book about a newspaper's *house style* as such: the journal's preferred spelling of words or use of punctuation. It is about a style of writing for newspapers – and it was/is full of advice relevant and useful to all popular writers.) In its original version it quickly became legendary in the newspaper world – a 'valued possession'. It was made available to the general public in 1981 and became the standard manual of tabloid journalism. Nine years later the original book was revised and extended to comment generally on newspaper English. Don't be put off by its (old or) new title: *Waterhouse on Newspaper Style* is full of practical – and witty – advice for EVERY writer. It's certainly one of the most valued items in my shelf of reference books

● *Marketing for Small Publishers*, Bill Godber, Robert Webb and Keith Smith, (Journeyman Press). Hardly light reading and not aimed at writers, but if you feel the need to understand what goes on (or should go on) with your book manuscript once it gets into the hands of the publishers, this will tell you all. Although the title says, '… for Small Publishers' the principles are much the same for all.

● *Writers on Writing*, compiled by Jon Winokur, (Headline). A marvellous collection of quotes from hundreds of well-known and lesser writers about writing – advice to young writers, originality, work habits, other writers, editors, etc. Some quotes are funny, a few are scurrilous, many are astute – and all are fascinating. It's a book for browsing in.

4

ARTICLES

- **Ideas for articles**

- **Article outlines/queries**

- **Structuring an article**

- **Taking saleable photographs**

- **Before going on holiday (or a trip)**

- **Articles – pre-submission**

- **Article acceptance/publication**

- **Liven up your writing**

36 Ideas for articles

An article writer is an *ideas-person*. To keep working, an article writer needs a steady supply of new ideas. Some, apparently without conscious effort, seem to have a never-ending flood of ideas; the rest of us have to sit down and work at developing them.

Here are some suggested ways of developing article ideas:

- List your interests and areas of expertise. Now cross-match them. If you *know* about e.g., statues and the history of revolutions in England, put them together and write an article about the statues of revolutionaries, as I did. I've even cross-matched management techniques and the writing business. (Next, maybe, the management of revolutions?)

- Collect newspaper cuttings – about your own particular interests, plus anything and everything unusual. Put your cutting/stories together in different ways to make a variety of articles; avoid the obvious, the unusual is always more interesting. (And don't overlook the popular 'Umpty years ago today' type of item. These always come in handy.) A tip: you will find more unusual, worth-saving snippets in the tabloids than in the broadsheets.

- The 'agony columns' in women's – and other – magazines can be a good source of ideas for articles. They identify the problems of real people. Advice articles on how to cope with similar problems will usually be welcomed.

- List 10, 12 or 20 'tips', or offer an 'ABC' of anything on which you are a mini-expert (or can 'mug up'). This is often a good way of providing advice on typical 'agony' problems.

- Capitalise on your own personal experiences. If you can't wait to say, 'You'll never believe what I saw/heard/did ...' or, 'D'you know, I ...', that interesting item which excited you, will almost certainly spark off a fascinating experience article. But make sure you have more than just the one anecdote.

- Just as you couldn't wait to tell friends about your unusual experience, they too will be eager to talk about theirs. Listen carefully, and then – while preserving their anonymity (even from themselves) – write about THEIR experiences.

- Encourage, don't check, your research digressions; *let* yourself be led astray, up that fascinating side-track. (If you're up against a deadline and can't spare the time to digress, make a note of the side-track location and come back to it.) Today's side-track may become your next article.

- Ask yourself the Kipling questions: Who? What? Why? Where? When? and How? (See Checklist 17.) These questions, asked again and again, as the initial answers suggest fresh questions, work well with everyday items – paper tissues, credit cards or pound coins – and help kindle your own interest in finding out. If you can interest yourself, you'll be able to write an interesting article.

- Take one of your old articles and rewrite it, for a fresh market. Never sell an article just once. That idea, those facts, can be used again and again, slanted to the needs of the next market. Similarly: take an article written by someone else, some years ago – and using the basic idea and the facts in that article *updated with more of your own* – write a similar article. If it was worth publishing then, it's probably worth republishing now.

- Open your mind to receive chance thoughts and ideas. Ideas are all about us, we just don't recognise them.

And finally, a caution:

Ideas are notoriously ephemeral. Once you've found your new idea, MAKE A NOTE OF IT. If you don't make a note, your bright new idea – developed from one of the above approaches perhaps – will quickly fade away.
If you're not immediately going to write it up – write it down.

37 Article outlines/queries

More and more editors are asking to see preliminary outlines or queries for articles, rather than the finished article on spec – even for short articles. Check your next outline or query letter against these points:

● The obvious – but too often ignored – question: is the article idea appropriate to the magazine you're offering it to?
● Have you got a good title? The editor may not actually use it – editors are often better than writers at thinking up titles – but a striking title will ensure the editor notices your idea. Keep the length down – a maximum of five words is a good target to aim at. (See Checklist 18.)
● Have you worked up a really good opening 'hook'? An article outline/query needs to include the first one or two paragraphs of the finished work. And remember: good opening paragraphs are usually fairly short – say 20-30 words. (See Checklist 19.)
● Does your outline list – usefully as 'bullet points' – at least half a dozen aspects of the subject that will be in the finished feature? The editor needs to know that the article is going to have some meat in it – and roughly what it will 'look' like. Arrange the bullet points in a logical and interesting sequence.
● If your eventual article is going to contain interview material – anecdotes, etc. – from different sources, make this clear, and identify at least the source types. (E.g., 'I shall include several quotes from three well-known widget-makers.')
● If you are approaching an editor with whom you haven't worked (much) before, BRIEFLY explain your *credentials* – if any – for writing the article. (Maybe you've got a good collection of widgets yourself, or you've interviewed several experts. Maybe Lloyd George really did know your father. Or even just, 'Been there, done that.')

- Have you taken, or will you be taking, photographs to accompany the finished article? If so, either briefly describe them and/or include photocopies or small prints of one or two samples. Check that the samples are 'right' for the editor – transparencies, prints, colour, etc.
- Can you fulfil the promise that your outline/query implies? (That is, if the editor likes the idea, can you deliver the goods – to the required standard?)
- If you are 'new' to the editor, have you previously had similar material published in other magazines? If so, enclose photocopies – no more than one or two sheets though – with the outline. If you've not had anything strictly similar published, enclose photocopies of your 'best' published article(s).
- Have you got the whole outline/query on one single-spaced, well-laid-out sheet of A4 paper? If it's more than one sheet – redo it. And don't forget the SAE. (But be warned, even with a SAE, not all magazine editors respond to outlines they don't want to pick up on. That's life.)

[WF]

38 Structuring an article

An article has to have a beginning, a middle, and an end. The beginning has to grab the unsuspecting reader and persuade him or her to read on. The middle has to hold the reader's attention, and the end has to generate a feeling of satisfaction.

But an article also has to have a *structure* of its own, a sequence which enables the facts and opinions to flow smoothly and logically. Check out these broad structures to find the one most suitable for your article:

- **The chronological sequence** – you tell the reader what happens/happened/ to do in strict 'historical' sequence. This will often be appropriate for an historical subject: the story of a campaign or someone's life. It is almost essential for a how-to article: first you do this, then you do that.
- **The circular sequence** – an article about an historical subject might start with a thrilling moment of action, carrying on from there to the end of the story ... and then going into flashback to tell, in chronological sequence, the story from the real beginning up to that moment of action.
- **The 'twin peaks' sequence** – a general-interest article can consist of a number of 'stories' linked only by a common subject. The

writer selects the two most interesting, attention-grabbing, stories. One is used in the 'hook', the other the end-piece. Start with a bang, and end with another.

- **The slow build-up sequence** – the contents of the article are arranged in order of growing interest, culminating with a real bang at the end. The problem with this sequence is the initial grabbing of the unsuspecting reader.

- **The 'pyramid' sequence** – you gradually increase the reader's knowledge, starting by reminding them of something presumed already known and then expanding from that. In a technical article, it sometimes helps to start with a list of several aspects of the subject and then expand on each of them in detail – including perhaps lists of subsidiary aspects and further expanding.

Whichever sequence you adopt for your article, it pays, wherever possible, to refer back at the end to the introductory 'hook'. Such a back-reference imparts a feeling of circularity – and hence reader-satisfaction – to any sequence.

Note: For detailed advice on all aspects of article writing, see my own, *The Craft of Writing Articles* (Allison & Busby).

39 Taking saleable photographs

Editors like complete 'words-and-pictures' packages: they don't have to search elsewhere for suitable illustrations. Your feature articles will therefore stand a better chance of acceptance if you can offer photographs too.

Despite the increasing use of colour, many general-interest articles are still illustrated in black and white. If offering black and white photographs, editors will want to see prints, sized at least 8in x 6in. (Larger, 10in x 8in, prints are better but cost more.) Many editors will now accept colour prints and use them in either colour or black and white, as they wish. For quality colour illustrations though, you need to supply transparencies (slides): 35 mm may be acceptable but the PREFERRED minimum size is 2.25 in square (120 roll-film).

Most of the basic principles of producing 'ordinary' saleable photographs are equally relevant to black and white and colour photography. Magazine illustrations don't have to be artistic so long as they are clear and relevant. And with today's 'do-it-all-for-you', foolproof cameras, it's hard to go wrong with simple illustrations:

- Decide on what the subject is. (That's not as daft as it sounds – the subject mustn't be tucked away in a far corner of the picture as in some 'happy snaps'.)
- Move in close – fill the viewfinder with the subject. (If the subject is a view, it helps to give *scale* if you dominate the foreground – someone looking at the view, perhaps.)
- Watch the background – avoid the clichéd 'tree growing out of head' shot. (Don't overlook the possibilities of bird's-eye or worm's-eye views – both produce good backgrounds ... grass or sky. A long-focus lens can make the background nicely fuzzy – move the subject forward from the background and focus tightly.)
- Get it sharp – almost automatic these days ... unless you shake the camera.
- Include people in the picture whenever possible – *doing* something, not looking at the camera.
- Ensure people are looking – or if there's action, the action is moving – INTO, not out of the picture.
- Compose your picture to utilise the strength of the diagonal, or make good use of the dominant one-third points (one third up or down, and one third in from either side).
- Don't tilt the camera a little 'to get the top in'. (If you must, exaggerate the tilt: make a feature of it.)
- Take vertical pictures vertically – the camera WILL turn on its side – and horizontal ones horizontally.

40 Before going on holiday (or a trip)

The freelance writer can often make good use of a holiday or other trip. There are possibilities of writing one or more articles about the place visited or, at the very least, picking up some snippets of information which will be useful later in some as-yet-unknown context. Possibly the setting for a novel or short story.

You will get most (writing) benefit from a trip by preparing in advance:

- Check state of batteries and stock of films for the camera. (Even if you only take 'happy snaps', these can be useful *aides-*

memoires for later writing.) If you use a tape recorder for notes, check batteries and blank cassettes for that too.

● Phone tourist information agencies and consulates in Britain for available brochures, etc. Overseas airlines too will often have helpful giveaway material; if nothing else, these will suggest things/places/events to watch out for. (At your destination, collect everything in sight: brochures, local attraction advert flyers, 'What's On' booklets, etc. – even if they're not in English. You can always get anything important translated at home.)

● Obtain a map of the area to be visited – even a relatively small-scale giveaway map will help you keep your bearings while moving around.

● Read (at least skim-read) one or more tourist guidebooks to the area to be visited. Make notes of anything noteworthy to watch out for. (It's often the tiny unimportant 'extra' snippets of information that MAKE a travel article.)

● If not already covered from the above, identify regional food and drink specialities – in the hope of trying them.

● Get hold of a novel or travel book about the area – to read on the plane, to get you into the right mood.

● Collect a sample copy of the airline's in-flight magazine – a potential market, if not for articles about the current destination, possibly for future articles about Britain.

● Contact the editors of magazines for which you have previously provided travel articles, tell them where you're going and suggest possible features. If you're on appropriate terms with the editor, maybe discuss things on the phone. Have they any special angle they would like to be covered? You won't always get a commission – more likely just an expression of interest – but at least you'll have broken the ice and your post-trip approach will be expected.

41 Articles – pre-submission

Your article is finished. Before you post it off, work through this pre-submission checklist:

● You DID write the article with a specific market in mind, didn't you? Different magazines have different requirements, different styles. The differences may be slight but they are always significant. To sell, you must write what the market wants.

- Knowing the market, is the article the *right length*? It's no good submitting a 1,500-word article to a magazine that never uses anything longer than 800-word, single-page articles. No, the editor will not drop that advertisement to fit your article in.
- Is the article as a whole an *easy read*? (See Checklist 13.) Or does the reader have to work at understanding what you're getting at? To ensure an easy read, keep your writing style simple and straightforward – short sentences, short paragraphs and no 'hard' words for which readers might need to consult a dictionary. They won't.
- Have you a good title for your article? (See Checklist 18.) Keep it as brief and punchy as possible: it's the first thing the editor (and hopefully later the reader) notices.
- Have you a good 'hook' – a good opening paragraph? (See Checklist 19.) If you haven't seized the reader's attention in the first few lines (25 words or so), you're never going to get it.
- Does the article round itself off neatly, with any loose ends satisfactorily tied up – and ideally, reflecting the 'attention grabber' used in the hook?
- Is the article organised in a realistic and understandable sequence? (See Checklist 38.) Do the comments follow logically, one after the other ... or does the article jump about like a flea on a mattress? Fleas are irritating.
- Does the content of the article live up to the promise of the title and, most important, stick to the point? There are few worse faults in an article than starting off on one subject and ending on a totally different one. Stick to the one subject; use the other for another article. Make sure too that you have enough *meat* in the article.
- Have you re-checked all your facts? Get just one thing wrong and you can guarantee SOMEONE will notice it, and tell the editor. Your name will be mud.
- Have you gone back over your article and polished it – trimming off the waffle and the repetitions, shortening the over-long sentences, clarifying the meanings? The best articles are never just written – they're rewritten. (See Checklist 21.)
- By the time he/she reaches the end of the article, will the reader feel satisfied ... or merely sigh and say, 'So what?' Your article must either entertain or instruct the reader. (And if it's instruction, it's got to be done in a pleasant, acceptable manner: you can't FORCE anyone to read it.) Would *you* want to read your article if it were by someone else?

● Does your typescript LOOK attractive? (See Checklist 22.) The editor's first impressions are really important.

[WF]

42 Article acceptance/publication

Every time one of your feature articles is accepted and published, you have effectively won first prize – in the competition to fill *that* spot in *that* magazine. Whenever you offer your work to a magazine or publisher you are competing with many of your peers. Only the best 'competition entry' gets into print. So ...

● Have you performed the essential, brief *Dance of Jubilation* at again/finally 'winning'? And told your best friend or partner? OK, two minutes celebration is quite long enough. Now back to work.

● Have you already started working on what next to offer the 'accepting editor'? Something like: 'I thought my article on ... in the last issue came across rather well; thanks for the sensitive editing,' is a useful introduction to your next offer – and getting it in quick means the editor hasn't had time to forget you.

● Did the editor retain the title or change it for one of his/her own? If changed, note the change: try to emulate this next time.

● Have you compared your typescript with the published article, line by line, word for word? Studying the changes made by an editor to your work is the best training you can possibly get in article writing. Next time you submit your work to this editor, don't leave those changes to be made – get it nearer right yourself.

● If your article is/was illustrated, what are the characteristics of the pix that have been used – why did the editor select them? (Maybe the rejects were all horizontal, or didn't contain people, or didn't concentrate on the subject – and those used were the opposite.) Check. And get it nearer right next time.

● Have you extracted and saved the original of the published article in your scrapbook? (You do keep a scrapbook, I trust? See Checklist 8.) In later years you'll look back in amazement/disbelief at your early work. Equally important: the scrapbook may give you ideas for other articles. It's also your most reliable reference source – you *know* the facts are correct, they're yours.

● Have you made several photocopies of the published article – before you stuck it in the scrapbook? You'll want them to send out to 'new' editors, with future outlines/queries, as samples of your published work.

- Can you offer a similar article – with a few different facts and in a markedly different style – to another magazine? Rewrite it while the idea is still fairly fresh in your mind, and don't forget, as long as the words are different, you'll be able to offer FBSR all over again. (See Checklist 90.)
- Have you made a note of the dates: when you submitted the article; when it was accepted; when it was published; and eventually, when you were paid for it? Such data is useful – not only just for keeping tags, but also to know when to chase an overdue decision/reply/payment next time. (See Checklist 94.)
- Have you been paid for the article yet? If you haven't been paid by a month to six weeks after it's published – phone the magazine publisher's accounts section to ask if they need an invoice before payment. (See Checklist 96.) If not, ask when payments are usually made.

[WF]

43 Liven up your writing

There are no captive readers. To be a successful non-fiction writer you've got to grab your readers' attention – and hold it. Take notice of advertisements. Many of the techniques used by advertising copywriters are relevant to feature writers. Like:

- Use an arresting title: short and punchy (five words is a good top limit). Most people glance at titles: only a few are hooked and read on. (See Checklist 18.)
- Where possible, use 'trigger' words and phrases to make people *notice* your titles – 'How to …', 'A New Way to …', 'Successful …', 'One-minute …', 'Ten Tips …', 'Sex', 'Money' (or 'Free').
- Remember – if you want to interest people, 'harness' your article-subject to MONEY, FOOD, SEX and HEALTH … and anything that relates to those fundamental topics. (This doesn't have to be blatant: the topic of SEX, for instance 'embraces' love, relationships, marriage, home-life, children, etc.)
- Vary the lengths of your paragraphs – but always keep them short. (Even the finest fillet steak has to be cut into fork-sized pieces for eating.)
- Link paragraphs together, to keep the reader reading: this can be by repeating a theme or catch-phrase from one para to the next, or by adopting a linking phrase at the end of one and the start of the next. (The simplest link of all is of course, 'And …')

- One of the most arresting words with which to start a para, or whole feature is, 'You ...'
- Irrespective of the article structure (see Checklist 38), always try to start an article with a bang – a real attention-grabber, a 'hook' (see Checklist 19). If you don't grab your readers immediately, you've lost them.
- Wherever possible, mention famous names within your feature articles – name-dropping implies endorsement. (I often quote from Mark Twain in my articles about writing – everyone recognises the name and I've adopted much of his advice.)

5

NON-FICTION BOOKS

■ Ideas for non-fiction books

■ The ten steps to becoming a non-fiction author

■ A non-fiction book proposal

■ Illustrations

■ Prelims and end-matter

■ Preparing an index

■ Assessing the likely readership of a non-fiction book

■ Children's non-fiction books

44 Ideas for non-fiction books

Many people have the makings of one or two non-fiction books in them. Many can write about their main hobby, interest or profession. After that, what next? To keep going as a non-fiction author, the writer has to come up, again and again, with fresh ideas.

Ways of developing new book ideas include:

● List your areas of knowledge, interest, experience (be as comprehensive and 'generous' as possible) and the various aspects of each of those areas. (Example: I know a bit about non-fiction writing; aspects of that knowledge include article writing, non-fiction book writing, photography for writers and the business side of writing.) You can perhaps write a book – as I have done on the above – on each of the separate aspects of your areas of expertise.

● Mix-and-match your different areas of expertise. (Example: as an engineer, with writing and lecturing expertise, I conceived the idea of a book about communication techniques for engineers; once a publisher suggested I broaden it out to be for all promotees into 'management', it did well.)

● Vary your target readership. Maybe you can write a children's book about an adult subject. (Example: one of my first books was explaining various public services – water supplies, road-building, etc. – to young people. And I'm longing to write a children's book about writing.)

● Study publishers' lists of forthcoming titles (check in your library for *The Bookseller*'s Spring and Autumn Books special issues), looking particularly for new series into which you could possibly slot a book on one of your specialities. (Example: having seen Dianne Doubtfire's *Craft of Novel-Writing*, I offered its publisher the idea for my *Craft of Writing Articles* – it was accepted, and those first two books became the foundations of the comprehensive Allison & Busby Writers' Guides series.)

● Think about the matters of permanent popular interest: health, money, sex, safety, parenthood, etc. (For others, look in any tabloid newspaper.) Can you research some aspect of one of these topics? (Example: I recently researched – from scratch – and wrote a book on home security. Inevitably, I called it *Safe as Houses*.)

● Can you think of a DIFFERENT WAY of re-presenting some aspect(s) of your expertise? (Example: the checklist format of this book is somewhat unusual.)

If your knowledge only extends to part of a subject you can often narrow down the subject (and title) of a proposed book to fit your expertise. For example, instead of writing a book on the Smith family, of whom you knew only Bill, make the subject Bill Smith. And if you only knew him as a youngster, suggest 'The Early Years of Bill Smith'. This 'focusing down' principle could be applied equally to 'things': Asian Antiques/Japanese Antiques/Netsuke.

45 The ten steps to becoming a non-fiction author

There are many more opportunities for becoming a published author of non-fiction, than there are for novelists. The process is straightforward:

1 Define the SUBJECT: What do you know about?
                          (Think title.)
                          Is the subject big enough?

Can you cover the whole subject?
Can you access the material you need?

2 Assess the MARKET:
Define the target reader.
Review the competition.
Identify a gap in market.
(Think globally.)

3 Complete the subject RESEARCH.

4 Produce a SALES PACKAGE:
Synopsis:
Think in terms of 10 chapters.
Think of 10 'topics' per chapter.
Think of 500 words per topic.
Think about the reader's needs.
Proposal statement:
Outline the idea enthusiastically.
Sell yourself – the expert.
Review and define the likely market.
(See Checklist 50.)
Discuss the competition.

5 Interest a PUBLISHER:
From Market Research (2 above):
Identify say 6 likely publishers.
Post out the sales package one-by-one
... WAIT ...
Eventually, when a publisher is interested:
Be flexible – not dogmatic.
Fit in with series, etc. needs.

6 Produce SAMPLE CHAPTERS:
Must be first-class – and 20 per cent maximum.
Include all relevant material.

Note: Unlike the sample chapters for a novel, which should *always* be the first two or three (See Checklist 67), to demonstrate the story development, the sample chapters for a non-fiction book can usually be 'author's choice'. (See Checklist

46) The first, introductory, chapter is seldom a wise choice. (But apply common sense: with a 'story-line' type of non-fiction book, the *first* two or three chapters, as for a novel, may be more appropriate.)

7 Negotiate AGREEMENT:	***Watch out for:*** Achievable length and delivery date. Usual royalties (10 per cent hb; 7.5 per cent pb.). Advance (50 per cent of first print run).
8 WRITE the book:	Write to timetable and word-budget. ***Write simple (never to impress):*** Short words, sentences and paras. Make it flow – read it aloud. Think always of reader.
9 DELIVER the manuscript:	Good professional presentation. Provide *all* material. Remember ... the index, to follow. Don't pester – wait maybe a month.
10 Help to SELL the book:	Copy-edit, revision, proofs, blurb, etc. Co-operate – for publicity and hype.

For more on all aspects of writing non-fiction books, check out my *How to Write Non-Fiction Books* (Writers' Bookshop).

46 A non-fiction book proposal

The 'proposal statement' for a non-fiction book is the most important part of the author's selling process. It needs much careful preparation:

● Have you thoroughly developed your book *idea*; is it big enough for a book – at least 30,000 words? (And even that's far too short for many publishers.)

- Have you come up with a really good, catchy yet descriptive, title for your book? A good title goes a long way towards selling the book to a publisher.
- Have you described the book – throughout both the proposal and its accompanying synopsis – in the best possible terms? Have you presented a good product image? Don't forget, you are going to SELL the book before you write it.
- Have you identified your target readership? Your book must be written for them – not for you. Explain why these target readers will WANT to read your book.
- Do you really know the whole of the subject *as you have defined it* for the purposes of the book contents? (You may be able to redefine the scope – or the target readership – of a non-fiction book to keep its contents within the bounds of your knowledge and experience.)
- Is there *room* in the marketplace for your book? How – specifically – will your book be better than those already published? You need to know all about the competing books to answer that point. (See Checklist 50.)
- Have you identified the most appropriate publisher(s) to offer your book idea to? It's not enough merely to identify one who publishes non-fiction; most publishers specialise in well-defined *areas* of non-fiction.
- Does 'your selected publisher' have any existing series of books within which your work might fit – and where there is an identifiable gap which your work could fill? If so, have you studied other books IN THAT SERIES and adjusted your approach – format, style, target readership, number and length of chapters, overall length, illustrations, etc. – to their pattern? (Many non-fiction books will sell best within an on-going series.) It's better to adjust your proposal to a publisher's needs than for your book not to be published.
- If your book can in some way be associated with an examination syllabus, double-check this to be sure, and then state the fact as a major selling point.
- Does your (2-3 page) synopsis show – in detail – how you will cover the whole subject, and demonstrate that you have enough material to fill each chapter?
- Have you outlined – without false modesty – your credentials (qualifications, knowledge, experience, 'connections', etc.) for

writing the book? This is the time to blow your own trumpet – and blow it loud. You've GOT to SELL the book idea and yourself as a package. Beware OVERSELL though – you must be able to live up to your promises.

- If your chosen publisher wishes to have two sample chapters submitted at the same time as the synopsis, market assessment and statement of author's credentials – as some do – are they complete, and really good?

  With most non-fiction books, it's best to choose the sample chapters on aspects you know well. Note that this approach to the sample chapters is very different from that for novels. With 'story-line type' non-fiction books, it may be wisest to prepare and offer the *first* two or three chapters, as for a novel. (See Checklist 67.)

  If sample chapters are not immediately required, tell the publisher you have chapters x and y ready, rather than wait for him to ask for his choice of chapters – which may not be the best for you.

- Have you identified the best/right contact person within the publisher's editorial department to address your submission/proposal to? Writing to a 'name' should mean more chance of the proposal being carefully considered.

[WF]

47 Illustrations

It is said that a good picture is worth a thousand words. Certainly, good illustrations increase the appeal of almost any non-fiction book. (Notice a reader's initial tasting of such a book – they flip the pages, searching for, and stopping mainly to look at, the illustrations.)

In any technical or How-to book or article, illustrations can be:

- Line drawings – including 'exploded' views of things.
- Flow charts – including 'word diagrams'.
- Graphs – including pictorialised tables such as pie charts, bar charts, etc.
- Maps – accurate, 'sketch' or diagrammatic (like the famous London Underground map).
- Handwritten notes, etc. – illustrating layout, etc.
- Photographs – of course (and always remember to get in close – see Checklist 39).

All such 'technical' illustrations can usually be produced by non-fiction writers themselves. If not, the writer should produce 'roughs'

– accurately scaled or dimensioned sketches – from which a magazine's or publisher's artist can work.

When producing one's own, basically line, illustrations, it is important to remember to draw them larger than their intended reproduction-use. Ideally, prepare finished illustrations 50 per cent larger than use-size. Remember, too, that when illustrations are reduced for printing, everything is reduced – line widths, incorporated text, numbering, etc.

In a non-technical, non-fiction book or article – biographies, travel stories, histories, and similar 'storyline' type books – other than for such things as family trees, maps, etc., line drawings are seldom appropriate. 'Storyline' type illustrations are more likely to be:

● Photographs of present-day things – including scenery, people, statues, gravestones, memorial plaques, privately-owned artefacts, antiques, etc.
● Photographs of artefacts within museums, etc. – not forgetting the archives and collections of major commercial firms.
● Photographs of events, occurrences, etc., in the past.
● Photographic reproductions of works of art in museums, galleries, etc.
● Reproductions of early prints (pen-and-ink drawings, etc.).

Other than photographs of currently and publicly available subjects, which writers can often take for themselves (again, see Checklist 39), most of the above illustrations will need to be specially obtained. Sources will include:

● Private or publicly owned museums and galleries.
● Newspaper (and Press Association) archives.
● Picture agencies and libraries – well listed in current editions of *The Writers' & Artists' Yearbook* (A. & C. Black, London, annually).

A crucial reminder: do not expect merely to pay the cost of a photographic print – you will have to pay a SIGNIFICANT reproduction fee for each illustration obtained from the above sources. The best course of action for a writer is to determine what is available, select the illustrations wanted, and arrange for the publisher to obtain and pay for the illustrations. (A publisher will sometimes specify in advance, in the agreement, how much he is prepared to pay in reproduction fees.)

DO NOT obtain illustrations in advance – there is likely to be a time-based rental for them.

48 Prelims and end-matter

Almost every non-fiction book has, at its front, a set of standardised pages – the *prelims* or *preliminary pages*. (Novels have fewer and less formally standardised *prelims*.) .

For non-fiction books the *prelims* consist of:

Page i	*Half-title*	a right-hand (*recto*) page containing only the title
Page ii	*Half-title verso*	a left-hand page (the reverse, or *verso* of the previous page, which is a *recto*). It may be used to list other books by the author, or related books from the same publisher.
Page iii	*Title-page*	a right-hand page containing the book's full title, with sub-title if any, the author's name (and relevant academic qualifications, if any), and the publisher's imprint/logo or name and abbreviated address.
Page iv	*Title-page verso*	a left-hand page containing legal and bibliographical information. It includes the publisher's name and address, the copyright notice and the author's moral rights assertion, the conditions of sale, the book's publishing history, its ISBN (International Standard Book Number) and the printer's name
Page v	*Contents page*	a right-hand page containing the chapter-by-chapter list of the book's contents.

Thereafter, the *prelims* are less standardised; there can be a dedication, an acknowledgement, a list of illustrations, and perhaps a preface. Such 'extras' however will be a matter for discussion with the publisher.

The prelims of a novel will always include – but not necessarily at pages iii and iv – the *title-page* and *title-page verso* with much the same standard content. The novel's *half-title* page is often used, particularly in paperbacks, for a 'taster' of the book or an author biography.

A book's end-matter is less standardised than its *prelims*. (A novel will have no end-matter.) In a non-fiction book it may consist of some or all of:

- appendices,
- end-notes (replacing expensive footnotes),
- a bibliography, and
- the index (virtually always).

Again, the end-matter should be discussed with the publisher.

49 Preparing an index

An index is an ESSENTIAL part of any non-fiction book. Consulting a non-fiction book without an index is like travelling without a map. First-time, non-fiction authors sometimes find indexing a difficult chore. The alternative is to engage the services of a member of the Society of Indexers – but many writers will find their (perfectly reasonable) charges more than they can afford. So ... we're back in a DIY situation. The following procedure will help to ease the problem:

- On the page proofs, identify (I use a highlighter pen) all important matters that you wish to index. (Some prefer, as I do, to index the manuscript first and then correct the page numbers when page proofs arrive.)
  - ◆ You will usually wish to index each chapter title (or a more explicit description of the chapter contents) and each sub-head (ditto) within each chapter.
  - ◆ Index too, all other important items (without sub-heads) and words within the chapters. Remember: the object of an index is to assist the reader to (re)locate information about specific points of interest. Where the preferred 'index-word' does not actually appear on the page, yet is dealt with, write the 'index-word' in the margin and highlight it there.
  - ◆ It is seldom essential to index every book and magazine title mentioned in the book, nor every place or proper name – decide first on the importance of each to the reader.
- List each identified index item and the page (or folio) number.
  - ◆ You will often wish to provide double entries – e.g., *Style, writing*, and *Writing style*. Initially, show the page numbers

in both locations. When finalising the index though, you can either retain the page numbers at both entries (my preference) or, for instance, at *Writing style* merely say *See Style, writing*.

- If preparing the index without a computer, have sheets of paper headed with the letters of the alphabet. Record each entry on the appropriate sheet. (At the end, the relatively small number of entries on each sheet will not be too difficult to rearrange in alphabetical order.) If your book is long and the index particularly complicated, it may be worth adopting the index-card system of indexing: a fresh card for each entry, alphabetically sorted by hand when complete. I have never yet found this necessary.

- Many of today's word processors include the invaluable facility to sort a list of entries into alphabetical order. If not, and you have access to a spreadsheet program, type your random-ordered list of entries as a single column of cells – any spreadsheet will sort such a column alphabetically. Many word processor programs will 'automatically' produce the index from identified items: this is a complicated procedure and the finished index will still need sorting out – the 'human touch'.

- However the initial alphabetical listing is produced, you now have to combine repeat entries: *Copyright*, 9 and *Copyright*, 78 should appear as a single entry, *Copyright*, 9, 78. You should also group linked index entries together. For example, initial entries of *Chapter content*, *Chapter length*, *Chapter start*, and *Chapter structure* would all appear in the index under *Chapter:* (note the colon) with sub-entries for *content*, *length*, etc.

- Study the index in any published non-fiction book – notice how the entries are set out.
  - Each entry is followed by a comma, then a single space, then the page number.
  - If there are several page numbers – usually, it's best to avoid more than about half a dozen page references per entry – they are separated by commas (and single spaces).
  - Blocks of pages are shown as, e.g., 113-7, or 113-22, not as 113-117 or 113-122. The end number is shown in the shortest possible form.
  - There is no full stop at the end of an index line.

- If you have prepared your index from the manuscript pages, you will need to correct all entries on receipt of the page proofs. I first highlight the page proofs identically with the highlighting of the manuscript. The task of finding indexed items and changing page numbers is then simple – and soon done. At proof stage, speedy completion of the indexing is always essential. The pressure is on. (One advantage of providing a manuscript-based index is that the publisher then knows how much space the finished index will take up. If you are starting the index at proof stage, it is worth giving the publisher an idea of the number of index entries when delivering the manuscript.)

50 Assessing the likely readership of a non-fiction book

On receipt of a non-fiction book proposal, one of the things a publisher needs to assess is the size of the likely readership. Can he sell sufficient copies of your book to make a good profit? (If not, why publish it?)

The publisher will look to the potential author to give him some indication of the likely market for the book; this information should be in the proposal document accompanying the synopsis – see Checklist 46.

To make your own assessment of the market, consider:

- Are there many up-to-date, competitive books? If there are few, are you the only writer who can see a market out there? Possible, but somewhat unlikely: think carefully. Check that competitors are up to date: outdated books may mean the subject is no longer of popular interest – who plays canasta nowadays?
- If appropriate to your book, is there a relevant anniversary to which to link the book's launch? (Anniversaries – birth, death, marriage, first publication, election, whatever – generate interest.)
- Are there any popular specialist magazines about the subject of your book? (Everyone, these days, is a computer nut: there are dozens of popular magazines about computing – and plenty of books. I know of no magazines about widget-collecting: it's therefore unlikely that many people collect them, or would buy a book about it.)
- Assuming a subject with popular specialist magazines, review the magazines' small adverts (both display and classified) – are there many? (If advertisers are making money from your subject, probably your book could too.)
- Is the subject of your book of interest to both men and women?
- Is the subject of your book of international or merely British interest/appeal?

- Are there local evening classes and/or clubs dedicated to your book subject? (If there are clubs and classes near you, there are probably more across the nation – potentially a big market.)
- What level of reader – primary or secondary school-children, children at home, non-specialist adults, enthusiasts, university students/graduates, working specialists/technicians/professionals – will the book be written for?

No one will expect you, the writer, to make an *accurate* assessment of overall readership, but the publisher will always welcome logical and well-founded advice. In the end though, the publisher will make his own assessment – and his own commercial decision.

51 Children's non-fiction books

As with adult non-fiction books, never write the whole of a children's non-fiction book until after you've sold the idea to a publisher. And:

- In choosing a target publisher, have you checked their recent catalogues – to determine whether they have a suitable, relevant series into which your book idea might slot – or whether they take one-off, children's non-fiction books? (Many publishers don't take one-offs.) Check the lists of other publishers too: is there a gap in the market for your book?
- Having determined that your target publisher has a potentially suitable slot for your book idea, have you actually studied one or two of his books similar to yours? (Usually, your book will need to fit the publisher's requirements – not vice versa.)
- Are you quite clear as to the readership at which your book is aimed? You can't merely think of it as 'for children': children come in various specific-but-woolly-at-the-edges age groups – 5-8, 9-12, teenagers; they each need addressing very differently. (And there may be opportunities for you to write a similar-but-different book for each age group.)
- Are you presenting your book idea – i.e., synopsis or list of topics – so that it demonstrates your awareness of the publisher's series requirements: standard number of pages, or of double-page spreads, treatment, etc? If a one-off, is it of similar length to other one-offs the publisher has on his list?

- Can your book subject be in any way linked with the National Curriculum? If so, say so – and explain how. (This can be a particularly good selling point.)
- Have you thought up a good title for your proposed book? (A title can go a long way to selling the idea.)
- Have you prepared a really good sample chapter and/or several sample double-page spreads to demonstrate how you will produce the final book? Particularly in books largely consisting of self-contained double-page spreads – as many children's non-fiction books do – it often helps if you can break up each set of topical material into a number of smaller 'bites': lists, statistics, would-you-believe-its, etc. Naturally, your samples (and the follow-up balance of the book) will avoid racism, sexism, ageism – and all the other '-isms'.
- Throughout the preparation of your samples, etc., have you borne in mind the need for illustrations? Non-fiction books for children have to be lavishly illustrated. (You won't usually prepare the illustrations yourself – but you must offer suggestions, artist's briefing material, etc.)
- Can you inject some humour into the book – and demonstrate this inclusion in the sample material? Even if you're not naturally a funny person, there will be aspects with a funny side which you should draw out.
- Have you the necessary credentials to produce the book you're proposing? You must be able to write knowledgeably and authoritatively, at least at the level at which the book is pitched. (You don't have to be a school-teacher, just know more than the readers.)

[WF]

6

I WANNA TELL YOU A STORY - I

Many of the techniques of fiction writing are common to both short stories and novels. There is therefore no obvious way of sub-dividing the fiction checklists in the way that the non-fiction ones were separated. So, to avoid a cumbersomely long chapter, an arbitrary split has been made: Chapters 6 and 7 should be read as one entity.

- **Ideas for fiction**

- **Plotting**

- **The seven basic story plots**

- **Viewpoints**

- **Conflict**

- **Show – don't tell**

- **Sensual writing**

- **Creating realistic characters**

- **Naming fictional characters**

- **Adult characters – biographical details**

- **Improving your fictional dialogue**

52 Ideas for fiction

Every writer needs a steady supply of ideas for the next short story or novel. Most of us have to sit down and work at developing them.
    Check out these methods of getting ideas:

- Read the blurb (the introductory lines, usually in bold beneath the title) – or just the title – of a published story ... and stop right there. Now, write a story to fit the blurb or title. Don't read the whole of the original story – just the blurb. That way, you can be sure that your story will be completely different.

- The 'agony columns' in women's magazines are always a source of ideas for short stories. They identify the problems of real people – readers. Readers enjoy stories with realistic problems and realistic solutions.

- Investigate your local history for ideas for your next novel/saga. Most places have their own (relatively) important historical personality. Background material on these characters will be all around you.

- You might find an idea for a story from overgrown local gravestones. A whole 'ordinary' family dying on the same day perhaps – WHY? (Play 'What if ...?')

- Investigate the 'Top Twenty'. Most pop songs are about love, and reflect the thoughts of young readers of *today*. Turn the theme of one of the songs into a story. Even the titles can spark off ideas.

- Keep your ears open for interesting snippets of conversation; you can always tell a working writer – we 'earwig' unashamedly, all the time. Overheard remarks can often provide the trigger for your next short story. Put your own speculative background to overheard remarks about the boyfriend, the vicar, the daughter, whoever.

- The 5WH questions (Who? What? Why? Where? When? and How? – see Checklist 17) can also help with the beginnings of a story-line – character, setting and situation. Then build on this. (Again, play 'What if ...?')

- Collect pictures of interesting-looking men and women, and of various settings. File for later use.

  Then, from your collection, choose pictures of a man and a woman and put flesh on their bones. Give them personalities, complete with faults and idiosyncrasies. Invent a dossier on each. (See Checklist 61.) Now put them together in a 'different' setting chosen from your files. Take note of how they react. That's the basis of a story.

- Let the train take the strain. Get on a train (or in a car – as a passenger) and let the passing scene inspire you. Play 'What if ...?' with fellow train passengers too. Exercise your 'imagination muscle'.

- Open a dictionary at random. Take, say, the fifteenth word in the third column of the two-page spread. Let that word be the theme or part of the title of your next story. If the word is totally unusable, repeat on another randomly-chosen page. Be sure it's the word that's wrong though – not just you being 'picky'.

● Sit in your local park, wander through the nearest street market, or loiter in the supermarket aisles. Watch out for an 'interesting' character: a 'bag lady' or dishevelled tramp, a harassed, but efficient mother and kids, or a lonely Colonel Blimp. Study your chosen character unobtrusively for as long as possible. Write a detailed description of the person and the setting. Now speculate about the person's background. Write this up too. Then play the 'What if ...?' game again. (This method is similar to that used by Alan Sillitoe when he wrote *Her Victory*.)

● Take a familiar nursery rhyme or bedtime story and update it. For instance, turn the Three Little Pigs into present-day people – a West Indian barrister, an Essex barrow-boy-yuppie and an out-of-work 'mother's boy' perhaps – who finance the purchase of their first house or flat in different ways. How would each cope with the 'wolf' – a property developer wishing to redevelop the area where they live? There, I'm really getting into it, already.

● Take one of your own *rejected* stories. Try rewriting it:
  ◆ as a picture-story script; or,
  ◆ if it was in the third person, rewrite in the first person, or vice versa; or
  ◆ from a different viewpoint; or
  ◆ change the gender of each of the main characters and then retell it.

And finally ...

Not another way of developing new ideas but an essential caution. Once you've found your new idea MAKE A NOTE OF IT. If you don't make a note, your bright new idea – developed from one of the above approaches perhaps – will quickly fade away. If you're not immediately going to write it up – write it down.

53 Plotting

Writing a story without knowing the plot in advance has to be rather like building a house without a plan, or starting a journey without knowing your destination or how to get there. Yet many successful novelists profess to having no more than a vague idea of what is to happen in their story, and 'travelling hopefully'.

Without doubt, unless a natural-born genius, the wannabe writer will be well advised to plan – i.e., plot – his/her story in advance: at least broadly. There are various suggestions on how to plot; what follows is an amalgam of some of the more sensible ideas:

- Before you can plot, you need to know your main characters – so prepare detailed biographies for them (see Checklist 61). You mustn't have your characters doing uncharacteristic things.
- Plot springs largely from conflict – see Checklist 56. The lead characters need not have just one problem to overcome at a time (except perhaps in a short story); they can have several linked problems on their minds, and preferably with several worrying them at the same time. By having more than one problem confronting the lead character at one time, one problem can be overcome while others continue to hold the reader in suspense.
- Every story needs a beginning, a middle and an end. The plot provides a shape to those three elements. For a short story, the shape may be little more than a simple rise to an all-resolving climax; for a novel, there should be the same on-going rise – but with plenty of minor peaks and troughs along the way. The multi-problem suggestion (above) permits a minor peak of achievement while maintaining the ensuing trough at a high level of suspense and interest.
- The plot is a plan of what follows what in the story; it allows you, the writer, to decide which character to introduce when; it serves to remind you to sow the seeds of the problems to come.
- In a large novel, you will often need a sub-plot – running alongside the main plot, possibly concerning secondary characters, ideally enhancing the main story-line.
- One of the best 'presentational' ways of developing a plot is either to use a single sheet, with the numbers 1 to 20 down the left side, or to take twenty separate loose-leaf pages and number them similarly. (The 20 is an arbitrary number representing future chapters. Depending on how you write, and how long the book needs to be, it can be varied – I suggest not less than say 12, and not more than, say 30.) The loose-leaf pages allow more room for added-in notes; the single sheet allows a better overview and is probably a good way to start. You can always expand from the single sheet to the multi-page effort. On the single sheet:
    ◆ Against number 1, write a few words on how your story opens.

- ◆ Against number 20, write notes on how the story will end.
- ◆ Against intermediate numbers, make notes of a few high-point scenes you have already decided on. You can amend the numbers if you position them wrongly.
- ◆ Put the plan aside for a day or so and spend some time thinking about the rising shape of the story and the essential 'hiccups' along the way. Think too about the 'clues' you need to sow early, to bring on later crises.
- ◆ Add in some more notes against numbers.
- ◆ Think about when and how to bring in the secondary characters – you can't introduce everyone in Chapter 1.
- ◆ Continue adding in scenes – bearing in mind the need for conflicts and crises to be overcome (without which, there is no story) – until you've filled in all the numbered lines.
- ◆ Now ... review all the 'future chapters'. Do any appear to be 'treading water' or mere padding? Delete them ruthlessly. You've probably still got enough chapters.
- So, at last ... you've got a plot, or at least the makings of one, for it will certainly need refining. But you can do that as you go along.

For more on plotting, see *How to Plot Your Novel*, Jean Saunders (Allison & Busby).

54 The seven basic story plots

Various authorities cite different numbers of 'basic' or 'original' fiction plots. Certainly, many (most/all?) present-day stories seem to bear a noticeable resemblance to earlier tales. Seven seems to be the lowest number of 'originals' suggested. These are – supposedly – they. Check them out – and note that they are all about people working through and surmounting conflict situations.

- Cinderella – after many ups and downs, the underdog finally gets a just reward.
- Achilles – the hero is finally brought down as a consequence of a fatal flaw.
- Faust – in the end, a debt always has to be paid.
- Tristan – the eternal triangle.
- Circe – inevitably, the spider eventually catches the fly.
- Romeo and Juliet – boy meets girl, boy loses girl, boy possibly finds girl again.
- Orpheus – the gift that is taken away.

55 Viewpoints

In any work of fiction, the story is told from a specific viewpoint. You can tell a reader about an incident from various viewpoints – and the resultant tales can be markedly different; the action is seen through different eyes and different connotations may be put on it. It is up to the writer to choose the best viewpoint for the story he or she is writing. Commonly used viewpoints include:

- **The omniscient ('all-knowing') viewpoint** (sometimes called 'God's viewpoint') – inevitably told in the third person. The reader is given the chance to see and know everything that is going on, in different places, and in the thoughts of all the characters. The omniscient third person viewpoint was much used in the past by such writers as Charles Dickens – but is less common today.

- **The single-person viewpoint.** Readers know only what the viewpoint character sees, knows, feels and thinks; they cannot know others' thoughts or about anything that happens when or where the viewpoint character is not present. This is one of the most commonly-used fiction viewpoints: it can be first- or third-person, with the third-person viewpoint being that most commonly adopted, particularly in genre fiction. Certainly, for short stories, the single, third-person viewpoint of a main character is much the best.

  Telling a story from the single, first-person viewpoint can be highly effective – it encourages the reader to become more involved and identify with the storyteller more completely) – but is possibly more difficult to do than the single, third-person ... if for no other reason than the problems of avoiding excess use of 'I'. (The single, first-person viewpoint was much used some years ago in the so-called 'true-to-life' short stories in the 'confession' magazines – where many of today's genre writers cut their teeth. It is much less used today.)

- **The multiple person viewpoint** is much used in novels. A chapter (or possibly just a scene) will usually be told from a single, third-person viewpoint – with other chapters/scenes having a different third-person's viewpoint, permitting readers to discover what others know, and are seeing and thinking. (Much of the benefits of the omniscient viewpoint without the potential for unreality.)

Dos and don'ts relating to viewpoints:

● Avoid changing a viewpoint without making the change clear to the reader by a fresh chapter or perhaps, at a scene change, by a line-gap (and wherever, don't do it too often).
● Make the viewpoint obvious right from the start of the story – don't leave the reader to wonder.
● Beware authorial interjections – their use is *really* dated.
● Single-person viewpoint stories should usually be written in the past tense; if the present tense is essential, use it briefly. (Logically, the person telling the story is too busy to be doing something else at the same time.)
● A *confidant(e)* is a useful character to build into a single-person viewpoint story – to provide the viewpoint character with otherwise unavailable information.
● Take care that a first-person story doesn't become egotistical.
● Beware having too many viewpoint characters – this can be confusing.

Note: the viewpoint has a different meaning when writing picture scripts (see Checklist 3). In these, the viewpoint is that of the artist (the 'camera') and the reader – and can be widescreen, normal or close-up, with a normal, bird's- or worm's-eye view. Still with picture-script, it is also best to avoid giving away too many of the thoughts of anyone other than the main character.

56 Conflict

Without conflict, there is no story. Fictional conflict need not be physical and many stories have more than one conflict. The essence of story-telling is showing how the characters surmount the obstacles, survive the conflict. There can be:

● Conflict between two characters:
  ◆ between partnered man and woman
  ◆ between two men over a woman or two women over a man
  ◆ between two people over differing ideas/attitudes
  ◆ between parent and child
  ◆ between neighbours
  ◆ between 'authority' and the 'ordinary person'

- Conflict against circumstances:
  - poverty
  - unemployment
  - traffic rage
  - accident, injury, illness, incapacity, old age

- Conflict with oneself – inner conflict:
  - guilt
  - remorse
  - conscience
  - self-doubt
  - character flaw

- Conflict with the environment:
  - against nature – storms, earthquakes, mountains, dense jungle, etc.
  - against man-made disaster – train/air/car crash, fire, sinking ship, etc.

And remember, while characters are coping with one problem, another problem may be superimposed. (For example, a policeman struggling to cope with a major traffic disaster may also have to cope with a disagreeing colleague – or his own self-doubt.)

57 Show – don't tell

By their nature, news reports TELL the reader what has happened. But fiction is different. The reader has been invited inside the mind of the viewpoint character. It is the task of the fiction writer to SHOW, rather than TELL, the reader – to allow readers to experience for themselves all the action and the emotion.

- As you write about a scene, view it in your mind and let your words reflect all that you experience – using all your senses.
- Reveal your characters' personalities by what they say and do, rather than by reportage.
- Prefer direct speech and the active, rather than the passive voice.
- Use the viewpoint of a minor character to describe something not directly involving the main characters. This should help it to come alive.

- Instead of merely stating the colour, the temperature, etc., offer a comparative description and/or the effects on characters, through their viewpoint, and in their dialogue.
- Avoid allowing the views, experiences, etc., of you the writer, to intrude.
- Only include small amounts of description at a time, let the scene, emotion, etc., be absorbed gradually.

58 Sensual writing

Many novice writers only invoke the obvious senses – seeing and hearing. More practised writers let their readers experience them all, so that their sixth sense comes into play and they can appreciate the atmosphere, the emotions, the realism.

Write so that your readers can:

- **see** the scene you are describing – not just the people, but the setting too. Is the sky clear or do clouds occasionally obscure the sun or moon? Big clouds or small? Wispy-white, or steely-grey and heavy with rain? How full is the moon?
- **hear** not merely the characters speaking in their individual voices, but the background sounds too. In a romantic scene, there would be the gentle murmur of ... yes, and from the waves too. The wind might stir the leaves on a tree to create a whispering chorus to the action. And even that well-known host of golden daffodils probably made a slight susurrus.
- **smell** the unique odours of place – and people. Cooking, for instance, more than almost any other activity, generates evocative smells. Walk past an Indian restaurant, a chippy, or a shop selling herbs and spices – and sniff. The smells are instantly identifiable. Similarly, there is a unique smell to fear; a unique smell to babies (different smells at different times, each unique); a unique smell to a steam train – even to a boiling kettle.
- **feel** the texture – the clothes, the skin, the setting. There is a special, tweedy feel to a sports jacket; a different feel to a silk dress. Take the hand of a young child; then that of an elderly person. Describe their different feel. Other, less obvious things have a feel to them too – like the crunchy, slightly sinking-in feeling as you walk across a pebbled beach to gaze at the surf.
- **taste** the food, the drink ... and the dryness of the character's mouth too. Think of the slipperiness of an oyster as you swallow

it; think of the crunchy roughness of salad; remember the uncon-
trollable slurp of spaghetti. But don't forget the other tastes too:
we *know* that the mouth of a struggling athlete must taste horrible.
Summon up from your memory the taste in your mouth immediately before an unpleasant interview. Recall too, the taste of a
lover's kiss.

59 Creating realistic characters

Each of us is unique. We are all different from our friends, relations
and the rest of the world. In fiction though, because every character
about whom you write is your creation, you must work to ensure that
they each come across as different. It's the unusual which makes the
difference.

● Borrow intriguing characteristics from real people (a nervous
  scratching of the elbow, your own paranoia about punctuality, etc.)
  and give them to your character(s). Combine several people's
  characteristics into a single fictional person.
● Many people have *characteristic* gestures (a tilt of the head while
  listening, perhaps) or 'turns of speech' ('You know' at sentence-
  ends, maybe): give your characters such differences. Just don't
  mention them too often.
● When all the world is avidly following the World Cup, or the test
  match, or Wimbledon, as a Tour de France fanatic, I'm *different*.
● None of us is all good or all bad. Even a saint might have a well-
  suppressed hatred of something or someone; even a villain may be
  kind to pets. Equally, we're not all raving beauties – nor as ugly
  as ...
● You may wish to give a minor fictional character a noteworthy
  difference: the waiter a limp, say ... or a lisp, or even a repeated
  catch-phrase. Just small differences breathe life into cardboard.
  But remember, most minor characters seldom need to be memorable.
● Where the reader will expect a character to have a certain type of
  speech or clothing (the rough-spoken workman or the black-hatted
  cowboy baddie) give them a surprise – a lah-de-dah voice or a
  French Foreign Legion *kepi* – just as long as there's some logic in
  it. That's *different*.
● Collect pictures of people – men and women, young and old,
  interesting-looking or 'ordinary' – and select an appropriate one

for each character. Keep the pictures pinned up over your desk – or at least in your 'character-file'.

● Also in your 'character-file' include details of each significant character (See Checklist 61). Try describing a character (in joined-up words) in the *first person*. It may make the description 'come alive'.

● You really have to enjoy writing about all of your characters. You don't have to like them, you can hate them if necessary, but you must enjoy writing about them. (If you don't enjoy the writing, why should the reader?)

For comprehensive advice on characters, there is no better book around than Jean Saunders' *How to Create Fictional Characters* (Allison & Busby).

60 Naming fictional characters

The names of your fictional characters can be very important: they give an immediate indication of the racial origins and type (bubbly or serious) of person, and their social standing. They indicate the character's age – or the period in which the story is set. They can sometimes tell the alert reader something about the type of story they're involved in. Check out these pointers:

● Names like Maud, Agnes, Edith, Poppy, Albert and even Frank and George are currently rather dated and suggest either older people or a setting in the past.

● Names like Sharon, Tracey, Kylie, Shane, Garth and Wayne are present-day and often a bit down-market.

● Names like Naomi, Esther, Reuben and Jake indicate Jewish origins; Roman Catholics tend to adopt saints' names such as John, Paul and Mary; people of West Indian origin often have names like Winston and Garfield.

● Names like Peregrine, Auberon, Lucinda and Francesca are unlikely names to associate with ordinary working people.

● The form in which people's names are used can suggest either authority or 'of-the-people' friendliness. Thus William sounds authoritative whereas Bill could live next door. Similarly with Anthony and Tony, Jonathan and John, Margaret and Meg (or Maggie), Elizabeth and Betty, Bess or Liza and Dorothy and Dot.

- You can generate intentional gender confusion by naming a character Leslie, Phil, Jo, Terry, etc.
- Relatively 'safe', 'timeless' names without racial or class connotations for today's characters include: John, Paul, Dave, Tony, Claire, Helen, Jean, and Julie.
- You should avoid having characters with similar-sounding or - looking names in the same story; similarly avoid many characters with the same first-name initial. (E.g., Sharon, Darren, Karen; Bob, Rob; John, Jane, Jean, James, etc.)
- Look for a variety of first-name LENGTHS – Pat and Christopher rather than Jack and Julie; Scott and Stephanie rather than Tina and John.
- For surnames, skim through gazetteers for interesting-sounding place names, take note of street names in distant towns, skim through the phone book for common names.
- Avoid, unless looking for a deliberate effect, using alliterative first names and surnames (Dolly Daydream, Paul Pringle, Fenella Fortescue, etc.)
- Beware the stereotypical name: calling someone Pedro Gonsalez is as unimaginative as having a character named John Smith or Tom Jones.
- Watch out for (unless wanted in, e.g., a children's story) surnames which cry out for unfortunate nicknames or which instantly conjure up a picture of the person. (A school-teacher named Winterbottom will inevitably be nicknamed *Frosty-bot*, or worse, by the children.)
- Generally, assure yourself that your characters' names *feel right*. (Avoid the Dickensian-like 'name-signal' though – a P.C. Nick-thief would nowadays be ludicrous.)

Essential reference books on names are *First Names First* and *The Guinness Book of Names*, both by Leslie Dunkling. The tiny Collins Gem *Thesaurus* also contains a useful listing of British first names with their French, Italian, Spanish and German counterparts.

61 Adult characters – biographical details

Full name (even though you may not intend to use it, it's useful to know):
Born (date in full):
'Star sign' (suggests personality characteristics):

98

Birthplace:
Lives at (full address):

Height:
Build ('petite' or, skinny, or not-so-skinny, or 'statuesque', or ...):
Colour of eyes:

General complexion:
Colour (and length, style, etc.) of hair:
Parents' names and occupations (?alive?)
Parents live at (town only, unless relevant):
Parents' other children (and if expected to be relevant, cross-reference)
Family relationships (not all families are close):

Education (finishing level and specialisms):
Occupation:
Ambitions:
Hobbies (including activity sports):
General health:
Favourite foods/drinks:
Self-image:

Dress sense (clothes often purchased from, e.g., BHS, M&S or Harvey Nicks?):
Favourite clothes (and colours):

Positive characteristics:
Negative characteristics:
Fears and phobias:
Bad or unfortunate habits:
Sense of humour (not merely 'good' or 'poor', but what sparks it?):

Financial situation:
Car (new/old, make, type, colour):
Home furnishings (just 'modern', 'twee', 'country' – unless an important piece):

Don't skimp on the above dossier: although you may not use everything, it's good to know the *whole* person. And now, check what you've got so far:

● Does your character's personality match their name?

- Will readers identify with (and 'like') the character?
- Does the character behave in a realistic fashion ... and feel 'real' to you?
- Have you successfully avoided a *stereotypical* character (and name)?

62 Improving your fictional dialogue

> *'What is the use of a book,' thought Alice, without ... conversations?'*
>
> Lewis Carroll

Dialogue makes a story, any story, come alive. Readers get to know and identify with the characters through their dialogue. And – a technical point – because dialogue is often in short paragraphs or even incomplete lines, dialogue generates *white space* in a book or magazine, making the text appear easier to read. But there are many more purposes of dialogue. It should:

- give the reader information
- move the story forward
- show the mood, emotions and/or personality of the characters
- recall past events and reveal future hopes
- help to create an atmosphere
- be used to build up suspense
- sustain reader interest and curiosity
- signal forthcoming plot movements

and often serve more than one purpose at the same time.

Finally, an after-writing checklist:

- Does your dialogue sound realistic without being mundane? ('Good morning. Pass the toast, please,' serves no purpose at all.)
- Have you suggested a regional way of speech but with only occasional bits of dialect? (An occasional 'Och aye!' or 'Hoots, mon!' is more than plenty.)
- Have you used colloquialisms in your dialogue, avoiding it sounding stilted? ('Don't ...' is more usual than 'Do not ...' and most of us say 'telly' rather than 'television'.)

● Are your characters' individual speech patterns consistent throughout the story? (Or do they all sound the same, using 'your voice'? Ideally, the person speaking should be identifiable without attribution.)

● Have you allowed your characters to interrupt and be interrupted? (We all interrupt in real life; so should your characters.)

● Have you used ENOUGH dialogue? (It's possible that you could transfer some description or 'back-story' from narrative into dialogue, improving the overall 'feel' of the story.)

Note: For more on dialogue, see Jean Saunders' excellent *How to Write Realistic Dialogue* (Allison & Busby).

7

I WANNA TELL YOU A STORY – II

Note that this chapter is a continuation of the fictional techniques explained in Chapter 6. Chapters 6 and 7 should be read as a single entity.

- ■ **Settings**

- ■ **Sex!**

- ■ **Story endings**

- ■ **Short stories**

- ■ **Fiction 'partials'**

- ■ **A twelve-part fiction synopsis**

- ■ **A 'CHAPTER' of essentials in children's fiction**

- ■ **Child characters – biographical details**

- ■ **Children's fiction – pre-submission**

63 Settings

Fictional action cannot take place in a void, each scene is played out in a *setting*. In a good story the reader gets to know the world inhabited by your characters.

- ● You need a number of settings for a novel – in a short story, a single setting will often be enough. In a novel, try not to use the same setting too often. Variety makes the story more interesting.
- ● Collect pictures – newspaper/magazine cuttings, your own photographs, etc. – of attractive urban and rural outdoor scenes, interesting interiors, etc. These will help you when describing the

setting of each scene. Ideally, know each setting personally – but that isn't always possible. The pictures are a good second-best.

- Choose a setting to match – or *deliberately* to conflict with – the mood of the scene. A bedroom or flame-lit fireside living room will be more romantic settings than a petrol filling station or a fast food restaurant.
- Ensure that every setting is relevant to the plot. (Don't include a setting merely because you like it: it must fit the story.)
- Don't describe *every* setting too thoroughly – leave something to the reader's imagination. You can create an *atmosphere* by evocative details rather than the broad canvas. Remember to evoke all the reader's senses. (See Checklist 58.)
- When your characters return to a setting introduced already, only mention enough details to allow the reader to recall the earlier description.
- The WAY in which you describe your setting – which aspects you choose to emphasise – can evoke mood, tension, drama, as well as the obvious image of place and characters. The same setting can be menacing at night, depressing in a rainstorm, or magical by moonlight; a farmyard may be a romantic setting – until the smell of pig-swill intrudes.
- Ensure that your characters act in a manner appropriate to the setting.

64 Sex!

A romantic novel would be incomplete without love scenes; indeed, most novels – not only romances – incorporate a relationship, and the occasional love scene. Love scenes can range from the chaste embrace and kiss, to all the sensual details of the erotic novel.

To write a love scene, a writer has to abandon her (or his) inhibitions and enjoy the writing. If you feel you cannot go into the detail necessary for one type of fictional love scene – write it at a different level, with which you ARE happy. In all love scenes though:

- Make sure that you show the couple ENJOYING it. (If they didn't, they wouldn't.) And show, don't tell. (See Checklist 57.)
- While avoiding energetic grunts and expressive moans, remember to include some dialogue – after all, people do speak while making love. (Even if only to say the time-honoured three little words.)

- Describe the FEELINGS of the couple involved, exercise the reader's awareness of as many of the five senses as possible.
- Remember that a love scene needs a 'build-up':
  - there will perhaps be a romantic dinner with nervous glances across the beautifully dressed table. (Remember the possibilities for 'special' background music, for 'special' drinks like pink champagne, and for the 'special' sounds of BOTH their voices. And maybe it's a dinner dance – your couple will be 'touchy-feely' close while dancing.)
  - there will inevitably be exchanging words of endearment, (Include them – even those ludicrous pet names.)
  - there will certainly be kisses – leading on to more comprehensive caresses. (Evoke ALL the senses in describing the kisses – the taste, the warmth, the pressure, the soft, gentle lips, etc. – and the caresses.)
  - and, assuming the love scene is to be consummated, describe at least the approach to the bedroom.
- If you prefer to stop there, so be it: there are still markets a-plenty for such tender love stories.
- If you accompany your lovers into the bedroom, there can be an evocative disrobing, followed – unless the urgency is by now too great – by further widespread caressing, hugging and kissing ... foreplay. (Evoke all the senses again, as above.)
- Again, you can leave it there and settle for a line of dots across your page, or you can go on to write an emotionally supercharged, highly erotic scene.
- If your love scene is in an erotic novel, it will have to be one of many such; as a rule of thumb, perhaps fifty per cent of such novels has to be sex scenes. You therefore need to vary the action as much as possible. Possibilities include:
  - In the bath or shower – all those slippery suds
  - In the open air – beware mosquitoes and intrusive grains of sand
  - the 'foodie' scene – exotic foods eaten from a loved one's body
  - being watched – peep-holes or one-way mirrors
  - ... and those are just the mentionable possibilities.
- Remember too, there are many more alternative positions to that supposedly adopted by missionaries. You will need to describe these.
  - Beware though, turning your erotic novel into a 'how-to' book: your object must be to titillate and describe sensually but without clinical details.

◆ And finally, in respect of erotic love-scenes, DO-O-O make sure that whatever activity you dream up is ANATOMICALLY possible – and correct.

65 Story endings

Irrespective of the occasional 'modern' story which merely stops, without any resolution of the conflict at the heart of the story, all the best stories have a beginning, a middle, and a *satisfying* ending. For the whole story to turn out to have been just a dream is NOT acceptable; for the conflict to be resolved by the protagonist unexpectedly winning the lottery is NOT acceptable.

The ending of your story must:

● be logical, believable and compatible with the motivations and personalities of the characters, and
● solve the problem at the root of the story, or
● answer the mystery around which the story revolved, or
● reveal the truth about a character in the story, or
● show that the main character in the story has changed, or learnt something, or
● relieve the tension or suspense which had been generated within the story, or
● clarify the confusion on which the story was based ...

and 'FEEL RIGHT'.

66 Short stories

You have written your short story – preferably for a pre-selected magazine market. Now check it out ...

● Are the characters in your story compatible with the magazine's readership? It's no good offering a teenage magazine a story about granny – even one of today's swinging grannies – or vice versa. Your main characters should be around the same age as the readership; readers like to be able to identify with them.
● Is your story the right length? More and more magazines are moving towards the short-short story – maximum length of about 1,400 words (and often much shorter). Individual magazines have specific length requirements: a hundred words over or under can

I WANNA TELL YOU A STORY – II

make the difference between rejection and acceptance. Check what they want – and conform.

- How many characters appear in your short story? There is seldom room for more than a (small) handful of characters. If you need a 'cast of thousands' ... write a novel. And a sub-question – are your characters alive, or just made of two-dimensional cardboard? (See Checklist 59.)

- Have you started the story *late* enough? Short stories can often be improved by deleting the first few paragraphs. Start as near to the end of your story as possible – at, or immediately before the crisis that leads to the essential *change*.

- Following on: does the main character *change* – develop his/her personality, overcome some diversity, learn something, perhaps as a result of the action in the story? The change need not be anything world-shattering – but it must be there.

- Still on the same general point: is there *conflict*? Conflict between characters, with the elements, with a conscience, with 'the way things are'? The shorter stories may have only a single conflict; longer stories perhaps more than one. But without conflict, there is no story at all. And the conflict must be linked to the change. (See Checklist 56.)

- Have you described your main character sufficiently for the reader to know and identify – but without a full biography (for which there is insufficient room in a short story)?

- Have you included some/enough dialogue? A short story which is wholly introspection and description is usually hard to read. Dialogue makes a story come alive; it lightens up the read – see Checklist 62. (It also makes it *look* easier to read.)

- Does your story-line/plot spring naturally from the characters – or is it forced, with the characters made to act out their parts like puppets? Plot should develop from character. (See Checklist 53.)

- Does your story start with a strong hook – and end with a *satisfying*, believable conclusion? (See Checklist 65.) And does the last paragraph leave a good taste in the mouth – without going into unnecessary details?

[WF]

Note: there are two excellent, complementary books on short story writing: Donna Baker's *How to Write Stories for Magazines* and Stella Whitelaw's *How to Write Short-Short Stories*, both from Allison & Busby.

67 Fiction 'partials'

A 'partial' is how many publishers now require an unsolicited novel to be submitted for consideration, rather than the complete text. From a 'partial', a publisher's reader can get a good idea of whether further consideration of the novel will be justified. A 'partial' consists of the FIRST THREE chapters – NOTE: not any three chapters at random – of a novel plus a synopsis. At the time of submission the author may or may not have completed the rest of the novel.

This list will let you check the likelihood of your 'partial' being approved.

- The novel itself first – have you kept to a single basic genre? If a book spans equally across two or more genres, it is less likely to sell – at least make one genre dominant. (And a genre first novel stands more chance of publication than does a 'straight' or 'literary' first novel.)
- Have you chosen an appropriate publisher to submit your 'partial' to? Not all publishers publish fiction, let alone books in all genres. And is a 'partial' their preferred form of submission for unsolicited fiction manuscripts? (Some, initially, will wish to see no more than the synopsis; others the full manuscript.)
- Are your first three chapters as good as you can possibly make them? They should demonstrate your ability to *develop* the story which is outlined in the accompanying synopsis. And they should *look* as immaculate as possible.
- Have you thought up a good, gripping title for your novel and ensured that your opening page(s) quickly 'hooks' the reader – in about the first 250 words? (You will also include the *sense* of this 'hook' in the synopsis.)
- Have you chosen an interesting and relevant setting (see Checklist 63) for your story? (Do you know enough about that location to write convincingly about it? If you get even the smallest detail wrong, someone will spot it.)
- Now more on the synopsis. Have you kept it as short as possible – concise – yet complete? Two or three close-typed pages should usually be enough for a typical short genre novel. (See Checklist 68.)
- Does your synopsis outline *the whole plot* – including the *denouement*? (You MUST NOT fight shy of telling the publisher the whole story in brief, including any surprise endings. The publisher won't disclose your secret.)

- Have you got *enough* plot – sufficient and ongoing conflict? (See Checklists 53 and 56.) Your story has to keep moving – and keep the reader turning the pages – throughout the whole length of the book. Don't forget to include sub-plots – they are often essential, particularly in longer novels. And the synopsis must demonstrate this plot-sufficiency.
- Do your characters *come alive* – and with lively dialogue – in the opening chapters and, importantly, in the synopsis too? Main characters should not be starkly black or white: most people are more grey. (See Checklists 59 and 62.)
- Have you identified a contact person within the publisher's editorial department to whom you can address your submission? Writing to a 'name' may give your 'partial' a better chance.

[WF]

68 A twelve-part fiction synopsis

A synopsis, plus the first few chapters of your novel – the package known as a 'partial' (see Checklist 67) – is all that many publishers will initially look at.

It is therefore essential to make the synopsis as impressive as possible.

One way of producing a tempting, persuasive fictional synopsis is to formulate it in twelve parts, each in just one or two brief paragraphs. Bear in mind too that the synopsis should read easily – a non-fiction-style collection of topic-headings is not appropriate. And yes, much of the first part of the synopsis will already be included in the sample chapters – but put it in the synopsis too, for completeness.

Beneath a heading consisting of the title, the estimated length of the finished book, a statement of its genre, and your (writing) name, describe:

1. The book's setting – place and time.
2. The main characters – their names, ages, professional backgrounds, etc. These, basically one-sentence-each, thumb-nail descriptions should include something special to make the characters come alive. Maybe a line or two of dialogue, see below.
3. The family background, wealth, status, etc. of the leading protagonists(s).
4. The opening conflict situation from which the story takes off.
5. The mood and tone of the story – ideally in just one powerful sentence.

6. The 'special ingredients' that are going to make your story unique. The theme(s) maybe.

7. The several continuing conflicts that make up the story – not in detail, but ideally just one or two powerfully written paragraphs.

8. Brief descriptions of some of the more important scenes to come in the book.

9. The ups and downs of the story-line as experienced by the main protagonists.

10. The decision-making scene, crucial to the whole story – the scene that changes everything.

11. The final climactic scene. And DON'T withhold the crucial denouement – the publisher NEEDS to know how it all gets sorted out.

12. The conclusion.

As well as the above essentials, it may be worth inserting, at appropriate spots, just one or two lines of typical dialogue from each of the lead characters; a couple of sentences of descriptive writing (part of a love scene perhaps), and a sprinkling of colourful phrases. It is also a good idea to repeat the book's title frequently in the synopsis – to hammer it home.

My thanks to Stella Whitelaw for allowing me to base this list on the 16 steps outlined in her excellent, *How to Write and Sell a Synopsis* (Allison & Busby).

69 A 'CHAPTER' of essentials in children's fiction

No matter what its type – picture-book, early reader or general 9-12-year-old story – all children's fiction requires the following attributes. And remember, virtually all of the advice on adult fiction applies equally to children's fiction. Check them out, and adopt the 'CHAPTER' approach ...

● **C – Characters** – Must be strong, clearly identifiable personalities, never 'ordinary', and can even be 'over the top' (see some of Roald Dahl's). They must, of course, be rounded and alive. Their personality should develop during the course of the story. Start with the characters and build the story around them. Child characters should predominate and where possible should be about the same age as, or slightly older than, the typical reader. Wherever possible, use the same third person child's viewpoint throughout the story.

- **H – Humour** – Most children adore humour, even/particularly the most *puerile* (hence the word). Introduce humour wherever possible. It's always useful to have a grown-up coming a cropper (again, see Roald Dahl's stories). Much of the humour should arise naturally in the way the story's written.

- **A – Action** – There must always be plenty of action, right from the start. There is no time in children's fiction for long, descriptive or contemplative passages. And remember, 'Show, don't tell.' (See Checklist 57.) Action usually occurs when resolving problems.

- **P – Plot** – There must be a good, strong plot, with lots of things happening: appropriate problems/obstacles being overcome, fresh obstacles arising; the whole story moving forward all the while. (See Checklist 53.) There is seldom room (certainly not in books for 6-9-year-olds) for much in the way of sub-plots. And the story must be rounded off – it needs a beginning, a middle, and an end.

- **T – Talking** – There should always be plenty of dialogue. Not only does dialogue help the story along, but it makes the text *look* easier, less daunting. Make sure that dialogue is: a) 'sayable', b) purposeful (i.e., free from waffle), and c) moves the story along. (See Checklist 62.)

- **E – Enthusiasm** – The story should always be told with enthusiasm, in a lively manner. (If you aren't obviously enthusiastic about your story, how can you expect your readers to enthuse about it?) It must never be dull.

  – Easy Read – All children's fiction must, as far as possible, be easy to read. Stories are not lessons – they should be FUN.

- **R – Relevant** – The storyline (and the writing style) must be correctly *targeted*, e.g., the right *length*, for the right *age-group*. It must be 'modern', that is, *up to date* in its treatment (even if about days gone by): today's children do not think/act/react as they did in the thirties or forties – or even the eighties. The story must be *honest* to itself – but it is NOT the place for 'preaching' or teaching – let the reader discover for him/herself. 'If you want to send a message ... go to the Post Office.'

Because of the strict constraints – lengths, reading ages, need for strong, logical plot, etc. – there is a strong case for always PLAN-NING a children's story carefully in advance. (See Checklist 53.) Work out the storyline/synopsis in detail before you start writing. Publishers will usually require a synopsis to be submitted with the book manuscript, anyway. (I work out a detailed storyline before I start and then write from that, varying the plot as necessary. Then, once the story is complete, I prepare another synopsis – of the story *as written* – to go to the publisher.)

70 Child characters – biographical details

Name:
Boy or girl:
Nickname/pet name
Address:
Age:
Date of birth:
Star sign:
Birthplace:

Usual teacher:
Favourite teacher:
Favourite subject at school:

Mum's occupation:
Dad's occupation:
Character's position in family: (Only child, youngest of 3, etc.)
Height:

Hair (colour, length, etc.):
Eyes (colour, glasses, etc.):
Face:

Best friend(s) boy/girl:

Likes: TV programme:
       Pop group:
       Food:
       Drink:
Dislikes: TV programme:
       Pop group:
       Food:
       Drink:
       Person:

Personality:
    (What is he/she *like?* E.g., tomboy,
    'fixer', 'swot', someone for whom
    things always go wrong, etc.):
Other characteristics, etc.:

71 Children's fiction – pre-submission

● Are you quite clear in your mind, which age group the book is written for? It's no good thinking it will be suitable for 'children of all ages' – ie, 6 to 60 – it won't. Children's books sell in specific age bands (albeit with 'fuzzy edges', to allow for different reading abilities): toddlers/pre-school; 5 to 8-year-olds; 8/9 to 12-year-olds; teenagers (often called young adults). The needs of each are very different.

● Is your hero/heroine someone with whom the reader can identify ... and preferably a little older than the reader? Arc all the main characters well rounded – do they come alive on the page? (See Checklist 59.)

● Have you incorporated humour? Children *love* humour – and especially if it involves an adult getting their comeuppance or relates to something that they consider 'naughty' or 'rude'.

● Have your characters got *today's* names? Not necessarily Wayne or Sharon, but certainly not Poppy, Winifred or Francis. Alternatively you can give them – and particularly the baddies – really 'over the top' names. (See Checklist 60.)

● Is your story *the right length?* Picturebooks are usually less than 1,000 words; most books for 5 to 8 year-olds are in series and around 3,000 words, but can go up to 7,000; one-off books for 8 to 12 year olds range from about 15,000 to 25,000; teenage fiction is usually around 40,000 words long. Specific book series have specific length requirements.

● Have you included in your manuscript, full descriptive details of all the illustrations – subjects, contents, treatment, and possibly an appropriate artist – you think should accompany your words? If so, **TAKE THEM OUT.** All you supply is the text; other than for picturebooks, leave the illustrations entirely to the publisher.

● Does your story start grippingly – with a good 'hook' – and speed along with plenty of action and dialogue? Children want there to be something happening all the time; there is no room in children's fiction for introspection, nor for long descriptive passages.

113

- Have you *read* much present-day children's fiction? If not, put your story on the back burner and get reading. Today's children's fiction is NOT like it was 50, 30 or even 10 years ago.
- Have you avoided, as best you can, all the *isms*? Racism, sexism, ageism, 'religiousism', and every other *-ism* you can think of. Publishers have to be careful not to indoctrinate children with unacceptable social attitudes. But equally, make sure you haven't been *preaching* – that's an unforgivable sin.
- Have you got a really good title? The title is of immense importance: work hard at it; it'll pay dividends. (See Checklist 18.)

[WF]

8
WORKING WITH EDITORS, AGENTS AND PUBLISHERS

- Contacting magazine editors

- How to get an agent

- What an agent will do for you

- Publishers

- Finding the 'right' publisher

- How to get on with your (publisher's) editor

- What to look for when proofreading

- Desk-top publishing (DTP)

- Self-publishing

- Vanity publishers

72 Contacting magazine editors

Whatever you write, or hope to write, for a magazine, it has to be approved and accepted by one person – the editor. The editor is responsible for the whole of the magazine's contents. Occasionally, the editor delegates authority for commissioning and accepting work to a fiction editor or a features editor. Check the magazine's masthead to ascertain who you should address. But whether in overall charge or a section head, editors are busy people. Don't waste their time. Bear in mind the following:

- The best INITIAL approach to an editor (or section editor) is in writing, with a fully-thought-through idea or a finished piece. Don't put up vague ideas.
- Address the editor (or section editor) by name. Phone the editorial office and ask the receptionist for the name of the relevant person to address.
- Always submit your work with a BRIEF covering letter – it looks professional.
- Always provide a large enough, sufficiently stamped SAE for the return of unwanted submissions. If you don't want your work back – preferring to reprint for offer elsewhere – then SAY SO, and provide an ordinary business (DL-sized) SAE for the editorial decision, or cheque.
- When submitting ideas for feature articles, submit no more than two or three at a time, each on a separate A4 sheet complete with your name and address – with a covering letter and SAE.
- When submitting the often requested samples of published work, always send photocopies – despite the SAE, the return of your samples may be 'overlooked'.
- Once you are known to an editor and your work is being used, some editors welcome phone queries. Identify yourself to the editor straight away – don't assume they will recognise your voice – and say what you want to talk about. Editorial staff will inevitably be in the throes of other matters when your phone call interrupts them. Prepare your question(s) before you pick up the phone, and be concise and specific, not woolly. Don't waste time: end the call as soon as you've finished. It's always a good idea to confirm agreements/decisions/commissions in writing immediately after such phone calls – to remind, or save the editor's time.
- Unless you are aware of the magazine's 'standard rates' (and despite what they say, these are nearly always variable), ask how much you are to be paid and agree this. (Once established with a magazine, do not automatically accept what you are offered – you won't get 'struck off' for asking for more money. Remember: those who don't ask, don't get. See Checklist 93.)
- Whatever an editor asks for and you agree to provide – provide ... as specified and on time. Honour your commitments and make the editor's day.
- NEVER ask for an explanation of a rejection. Even the most experienced writer occasionally gets them. You can't win 'em all. It's the editor's prerogative.

- When an editor moves on to another magazine, make contact with him/her there and seek to maintain your past working relationship. Get to know the new editor of the magazine as soon as possible too: re-establish your credentials and reputation – and even perhaps re-offer any ideas the previous editor didn't like (so long as they are still really relevant).

73 How to get an agent

Many publishers will only consider novels from 'new-to-them' authors if submitted through an agent. (This is partly to save the time and expense of sifting through hundreds of unsuitable novels in the hope of finding the few worth considering.) But, until a publisher is interested in your work, it is often as difficult to find an agent to take you on as it is to find a publisher. These suggestions should help:

- Study the lists of agents in the current issue of one of the standard writers' year-books; look for those who are full members of the Association of Authors' Agents (AAA). They aren't *necessarily* better than non-members but they will have reputations to preserve ... and a code of practice to which to adhere. Identify the specialities of the selected agents – match these with your own.
- Discuss their agents with other writers. Discover those with whose performance the writers are pleased. 'Star' these agents in your list of possibles. Will a writer friend introduce you to their agent?
- Take advantage of any opportunity to hear talks by agents – at conferences, literary festivals, etc. – and, assuming you like what they say, make yourself known to them and ask if they will look at your work. Some agents will tell you that they are not taking on new clients – but these agents are unlikely to be addressing writers' groups. And any agent will make room for a potential high-earning author. If they agree to look at your work, get in quick, before they forget meeting you. (This is one of the occasions when it is useful for a writer to have a business card.)
- If, as above, you are lucky enough to meet an agent at a conference, etc., don't be selfish – don't monopolise them for more than a few minutes. Remember that there are probably other writers also seeking an opportunity for a brief meeting.
- Apart from face-to-face contact, above, it is wise to check whether the agents on your preferred list are willing to consider new clients. Check this willingness – usually by a quick phone call, but

some agencies (identified in the year-books) prefer a short letter of enquiry.

● Whether enquiring about willingness to take on new clients or submitting a work sample, the covering letter should (more briefly in a preliminary enquiry, more comprehensively when accompanying a manuscript):

♦ be succinct and enthusiastic

♦ explain the nature of your current writing work

♦ indicate where you see yourself going with your writing – your plans

♦ incorporate a brief writing biography (See Checklist 85.)

♦ enclose an appropriately sized stamped addressed envelope

● Agents vary in their preferences for the submission of work. These preferences vary from the usual first two or three chapters of a novel plus a synopsis (see Checklists 67-8), to a complete novel plus synopsis, and, for non-fiction, either a detailed synopsis plus market appraisal and author's credentials or the same plus two sample chapters. Some agencies – not members of the AAA – charge an initial reading fee which is usually refunded once the book is placed with a publisher.

● It is not considered good practice to approach more than one agent at a time.

● Once an agent has expressed a willingness to represent you, but before finalising the relationship, it is wise to clarify just how the agency operates, its exclusivity requirements, etc., and its terms for both UK and overseas contracts.

74 What an agent will do for you

The primary role of a literary agent is to look after the commercial interests of their clients – to be their 'agent'. Literary agents act on behalf of their clients and are, effectively, paid by them – they deduct a percentage from the clients' earnings. Virtually all of a literary agent's income comes from their clients.

A good agent:

● has a wide and up-to-date knowledge of the publishing industry – including which publisher is currently in the market for which types of book.

● has good personal contacts and relationships with a number of editors – is not 'in the pocket' of any one publisher.

- has a good idea of what a client's work is worth in the publishing market-place at any time – and can thus negotiate authoritatively.
- will strive to get the best terms possible for the client. (Remember: the agent is paid a percentage of the client's earnings, so the better the terms, the larger the agent's fee.)
- will remove from the client, the burden of financial negotiation with publishers. The client can get on with the writing, secure in the knowledge that the agent is looking after his or her best interests.
- can give editorial guidance to a client – can help a client to make a 'nearly-but-not-quite-there' manuscript saleable. (A fresh look by a friendly 'outsider' can be immensely valuable. A famous writer once said that writing a novel is like building a house with one's nose pressed up against the brickwork.) An agent can help a client to produce the best possible work – by giving the *right* encouragement.
- can be a good friend to his/her clients, encouraging them through bad times (even, sometimes, those not associated with the client's writing activities), offering a shoulder for the client to lean and/or cry on.
- will check royalty statements, prepare invoices, chase overdue payments, check payments against statements, and ensure that the client's various rights are preserved and/or sold as appropriate. Payments are of course forwarded expeditiously.
- will often be able to suggest what a client should write next – a different area of work perhaps. Agents often sense which way the book world is moving … but are seldom infallible in this respect.
- will, within reason, be prompt in responding to a client's letters or phone calls and will always be honest and straightforward in their response.
- will tell a client when he/she has given up trying to place a particular piece of the client's work, will tell the client where the work has been unsuccessfully offered, and will authorise the client to attempt further marketing themselves.

An agent **cannot be expected** to sell unsaleable work. Few agents will market a client's short stories. An agent cannot be expected to offer detailed advice on unsuitable work or to give financial assistance to a temporarily embarrassed client.

75 Publishers

Mainstream – as opposed to vanity and self – publishers can be large or small organisations, household names or 'Who?'. They all, though, have one thing in common: they take all the financial risks of publishing your book – and they pay you for it. It is useful for a writer to be aware of what a publisher does with/to/for your book. And this is, inevitably, an incomplete list:

- He will make a decision on the literary merit of your book – is it WORTH publishing? But literary merit is not enough.
- From his knowledge of the publishing world, he will assess the market for your book – is there a demand or need for it?
- He will assess the commercial viability of your book. He's in business to make money – he can't afford deliberately to make a loss, although of course, he doesn't always get it right. (The commercial viability of a book can be influenced by various factors: illustrations to be obtained or prepared; permissions, etc., needed for quotations; likelihood of attracting good – or adverse – publicity; the marketability – which may include the personality – of the author; the likelihood of further books from the same author.)
- Having determined that, overall, it is worth publishing, he will arrange for the financing of your book – that is, he will put up the money. You get a contract (agreement) – and are paid an advance against future royalties.
- He will arrange, in-house or freelance, for the book to be edited.
- He will arrange for both the book's cover and its page layout to be designed. A tiny variation in the size or choice of font or the distance between lines (the 'leading') can make a difference of a whole signature (16 book pages) – and a significant variation in the cost.
- He will arrange for the necessary ISBN to be obtained and registered.
- He will arrange for the book to be typeset – a process linked with the page layout design.
- He will arrange for comments (not just the author's) on the book proofs to be collated and corrections made.
- He will arrange for the book's cover and pages to be printed and bound together.
- He will arrange for publicity – advance information, catalogue entries, review copies (and the statutory deposited copies), flyers, advertisements perhaps, and maybe author-involvement (interviews, signings, etc.).
- He will arrange for a sales force to call regularly on bookshops and, at least initially, push them to take stocks of your book.
- He will arrange for the bulk of the copies of your book to be warehoused, available to meet further orders.

- He will, in many cases, seek to sell further rights in your book – paperback rights, serialisation rights, overseas rights, etc.
- He will maintain accurate records of the sales of your book and arrange for regular payments of royalties to you.
- If and when the book's initial print run is sold, he will decide whether and when to arrange a further printing. (He will usually defer a reprint until 'dues' – unfilled book orders – have built up.)

Non-sexist note: because most publishers are men, I have used 'he' throughout this listing, but mean no disrespect to the many excellent lady publishers.

76 Finding the 'right' publisher

Offering a 'how-to' book to Harlequin Mills & Boon would be futile; as would offering a romance novel to How To Books. But identifying the most appropriate publisher(s) to offer your new book to needs a finer touch than such obvious differentiation. The ideal is to find the one publisher for whom your book is exactly right – and who is searching for something just like it. In practice, you can only hope to narrow down to a handful of publishers who might be interested in it.

The following steps will help you find the most appropriate publishers:

- From the annual writers' handbooks, make a list of publishers who mention the type of your book (fiction and genre, non-fiction and broad subject, adult or child reader).
- Look at the books on your own shelves at home – in the same fiction genre or on the same non-fiction subject. These books have appealed to you: who publishes them? 'Star' these publishers in your list.
- Visit your local library and bookshop(s) and browse through the shelves of books similar to yours. Identify the publishers who have *most* of the similar books – but also take note of the smaller publishers with just one or two similar books. (You will hope to be taken on by the larger publishing house but may not be lucky; you may stand more chance with a smaller publisher with a specialist interest – which can apply to both non-fiction subjects and fiction genre.) 'Star' these publishers in your list.
- Ask your friendly librarian (or, in a slack shopping period, you might try asking the proprietor or manager of a small bookshop)

if you can see a copy of the latest (or not too out-dated) 'Buyers' Guide to the Spring or Autumn Books' bumper issue of *The Bookseller*. (This is an inch-thick six-monthly publication; half of the book is taken up with listing, by fiction genre and non-fiction subject, the books to be published by most publishers in the next six months. The rest of the book is filled with publishers' advertisements – listing their new books for the next six months.) Again, identify those publishers likely to be interested in your book.

- With luck (and care) you will by now have 'starred' or otherwise whittled down your initial list of suitable publishers to a dozen or less. Phone each of them and ask for a copy of their current catalogue. (By phoning them you can often avoid having to provide a stamped addressed envelope. At the same time, it's worth asking the name of the editor in charge of the list-section you're interested in. You'll need the name later.) The catalogues will give you an even better idea of the books they publish; you should be able to narrow your 'attack list' down even more.

- At the right time of year, another way of collecting publishers' catalogues is to visit the annual London International Book Fair (usually in late March). Entrance is not cheap but once in, you will find that almost every UK publisher (and many foreign publishers) has a stand there. You will be able to collect catalogues and inspect books similar to yours. You may possibly be able to talk to people on the stands about your book but the Fair is for book buyers and most stands are manned by the sales team rather than editorial people. Few authors go to the Fair – but I've found it worthwhile.

- Your list of potential publishers should now be manageable – and as *sensible* as you can make it.

77 Surviving copy-editing

A publisher's copy-editor (sometimes known as a line-editor) checks a manuscript in detail for sense, consistency, grammar, syntax (sentence structure), punctuation and spelling. The job of a magazine's sub-editor is much the same.

Regrettably, writers vary from the precise and pedantic to the lazy and semi-literate. The precise writer will neither wish nor need corrections to his or her manuscript – but can have the odd 'blind

spot'. The lazy writer may rely on a copy-editor to knock unpunctu-
ated and misspelt work into shape.

Unfortunately and inevitably, copy-editors too can range from
repressed wannabe writers who by their ham-fisted 'editing' can
totally change a writer's style, to precise but flexible experts who are
a godsend to any writer. Even the best of writers is sometimes too
close to his/her work to spot the last few typos, left-over repetitions
or redundant commas.

To 'survive' copy-editing:

- Ensure that your agreement includes provision for you to see your
  copy-edited manuscript before it goes for typesetting. If the agreement has no such provision, INSIST on its inclusion.
- Before delivering your manuscript, effectively do your own copy-
  editing. Ideally, set your work aside for a few weeks while you do
  something completely different, so that you can come to it with
  'fresh eyes'.
- Slowly, read your manuscript through, checking that each
  sentence makes sense and contains no spelling or punctuation
  errors. Does it say exactly what you intended? Be sure that
  Belinda Blue-eyes, introduced on page 2, has not become Bella
  Brown-eyes from page 99 onwards. If you do this personal copy-
  edit well, there should be little need for many changes in the
  publisher's offices – unless you've got 'the copy-editor from
  Hell'.
- When copy-edited, look carefully at the editorial changes: most
  times they will be valid points that had escaped your notice.
  Sometimes they will be the rewording of a sentence, the meaning
  of which, in the original, was somewhat confused; make sure
  though that the copy-editor's rewording of the offending sentence
  has not changed the intended meaning. (A reworded sentence may
  be clear and syntactically sound – and yet be subtly incorrect in its
  meaning. The copy-editor may not understand – but has done the
  best she can, unintentionally distorting the message.)
- We can all make 'mistakes' in inconsistencies: have you hyphen-
  ated every 'copy-editor' or capitalised every 'How-to'? And have
  you no 'blind spots'? 'Its' or 'it's' are classic; colons and semicolons are a perpetual problem, and I confidently misspelt
  desparate for many years. (I know now: it's DESPERATE.)
- Also, just because the copy-editor's changes are not strictly necessary, do not reject them out of hand: they may be an improvement
  on your original text, and you've been 'too close' to notice.

- If you have, intentionally, written some parts of your manuscript in a way that will grate upon a copy-editor's sensitivity, tell your publisher so when delivering the book. (I include a few notes on layout, points to watch, etc. with every non-fiction book typescript.)

78 How to get on with your (publisher's) editor

If you are a book writer, your main contact within your publisher's office will be your editor. This editor may, or may not, be known as a commissioning editor but will at least some of the time wear a different hat from the copy-editor. Your editor is the person you will tell if your already-commissioned book is running late, if you want to change the title or if you're simply stuck. Your editor will be the person who has championed your book through from synopsis to acceptance and on to publication.

Your relationship with your editor is important – to both of you. To ensure as good a relationship as possible, you should:

- be reasonable, polite, straightforward and businesslike at all times – and expect the same treatment in return. If at all possible, be friendly too. (Send your editor a Christmas card.)
- write your best book possible: be sure that it warrants the time and effort the editor will be putting into it – something that they, as well as you, will be proud to be associated with.
- honour your promises – dates, deliveries, lengths, etc. – and be sure not to promise what you cannot fulfil.
- if you think something is going wrong, or that you are being ignored or wrongly over-ruled, say so, clearly but politely – and expect to sort it out in discussion. Check your agreement first though: some matters are in the publisher's sole discretion.
- discuss any necessary changes in your (non-fiction) book's content and organisation with the editor and thereafter keep to any agreed variations. (It helps to record such agreements, in a letter.)
- keep your editor fully aware of your progress – but without unnecessarily bothering him/her with minutiae.
- Leave your editor to get on with the job – don't chivvy him/her unnecessarily for comments or decisions. But against that if, for instance, after manuscript delivery, you hear nothing for several weeks, feel free to chase.
- turn around edited manuscripts, proofs, requests for indexes, etc., as quickly and efficiently as possible.

- try to work with, rather than against, your editor in editing matters and in any rewriting AGREED to be necessary – and be as flexible as possible when rewriting is suggested.
- remember to say thanks when your editor does you a favour. And don't ask for too many.
- finally, thank and congratulate the editor on the good job done in producing a successful book. (And then ask about the next one.)

79 What to look for when proofreading

Whether your book is fiction or non-fiction, you will be required to check the proofs – the typesetting of your text – prior to printing. The most important point to remember is that

PROOFS ARE FOR CORRECTING – NOT FOR RE-THINKING

Forget all those tales of the famous writers of the past who rewrote their works in the proofs. Do that today and you'll face a huge bill from the publisher. (Look at your agreement: typically, authors are charged for corrections that cost in excess of 10 to 12 per cent of the total initial cost of typesetting. That doesn't mean you can change 10 per cent of the text: corrections cost *MUCH* more than the initial typesetting.)

Particular faults to watch out for when proofreading:

- misspelt words – particularly the correct letters in the wrong order (These *typos* can be carried over from author's text on disk or generated by typesetter working from typescript.)
- paragraph starts incorrectly inserted or omitted (This seems to be a fault most likely to occur when the typesetters are working from an author's ASCII files.)
- missing or repeated lines (This used to be a common fault when an author's typescript had to be rekeyed by the typesetter. With texts on computer disks, it is now uncommon – except at page breaks.)
- missing or changed punctuation marks, and/or the space thereafter
- missing or incorrect italicising (or emboldening)
- excess (ugly looking) or insufficient (hard to read) space between words in a line (An author's typescript is best provided *unjustified* – i.e., 'ragged right' – which the typesetter then sets *justified*, and may squeeze or expand to fill the line.)

- inappropriate editing changes made by the publisher's copy-editor without the author's awareness (An author should – and nearly always will – see, and have the opportunity to comment on, the copy-edited typescript before it goes for typesetting: see Checklist 77. Check your agreement for confirmation of this.)
- page numbers needing correction. (In typescript the book page numbers are not known – the '00' has to be replaced, in the proofs, with the actual page number.)

And, don't forget that, once page proofs have been provided, the non-fiction author will have to prepare the ever-essential index. (See Checklist 49.)

80 Desk-top publishing (DTP)

Desk-top publishing is a misnomer. Even in its finest examples, desk-top publishing does no more than produce ready-to-be-photographed, book-like pages of printed text. Any powerful word processor will probably be all you need to produce simple documents and booklets; they are not sufficient to produce a professional-looking full-length book.

To use DTP as part of the process of self-publishing (see Checklist 81) you should have:

- a *professional* desk-top publishing program such as PageMaker, Ventura or QuarkXPress – this will cost several hundred pounds. (There are some much cheaper so-called DTP programs but ... you usually get what you pay for.)
- an up-to-date PC (or Mac) computer with a Pentium or better processor, a roomy hard disk and at least 16 Mb of *spare* RAM. (Of course, this specification is becoming easier to meet with every passing price-cut and computer improvement.)
- a laser printer offering an absolute minimum resolution of 600 dots per inch – twice that is better.
- training. There is a steep learning curve on DTP programs; it is wise to do a formal training course in the program you've chosen.

And even with the best equipment, much training and lots of practice, what do you end up with? A batch of beautifully printed single sheets – ready to go to the printer. There's a lot more to publishing than that – see Checklist 75.

81 Self-publishing

Self-publishing – which is not the same as vanity publishing (see Checklist 82) – is no new phenomenon. At some stage in their careers, Charles Dickens, Jane Austen, Zane Grey, Beatrix Potter, Rudyard Kipling and Honoré de Balzac, to name but a few, self-published their work. It should not though, be a first choice for any writer today.

Self-publishing entails not only a significant financial investment, but also a large amount of non-writing work. It will nearly always be better to find a 'mainstream' publisher to take the financial risks and do all the non-writing work. (See Checklist 75.)

However, some written work almost has to be self-published if it is to see the light of day. Few poets achieve commercial publication; few 'mainstream' publishers will be interested in the history of a small village or the like; few publishers are interested in narrowly specialist subjects with a limited market. These are ideal subjects for self-publishing. Novels – which need a large audience/market deriving from much bookshop exposure – are not.

If you are determined on self-publishing, an early decision is needed on the type of publication: a small, photocopier print-run of staple-bound typed (or word-processed) pages need entail no major effort or expense; a commercially typeset and printed paperback is a totally different kettle of fish.

The following checklist relates to the latter type of self-publication.

- First, assess the potential market (and the competition) as realistically (pessimistically) as possible. Can you *access* that market?
- Think carefully about your book. How long do you intend it to be? Your book must *look* like a book – if it is to have a perfect-bound spine, an adult book needs at least 30,000 words. A saddle-stitched book is best at least 48 pages long – say 15,000 words. Can you write that many words on your subject? (Refer to the several Checklists – 44 to 51 – on planning and organising a conventional non-fiction book.)
- Get *preliminary* quotations from a friendly printer for the cost of production.
- From the printing cost estimates, work out your total likely expenditure. Have you got that sort of readily available cash? If not, can you find someone to finance you? (Don't just be optimistic.)
- Make an assessment of the price at which the book will have to be offered. Remember to allow for booksellers' discounts, for advertising, for your own distribution costs (you may have to post

copies to advert responders). As a rough guide, commercial publishers price their books at five or six times the unit production cost; self-publishers can often work on around three times – because of their smaller overheads.

● Review your earlier assessment of the market: will it still be there ... at the now determined price? (Don't adopt a lower price in the hope of selling more copies.) You should plan, at the very least, on recouping your expenditure.

● Once you've got the market and the finance sorted out in your mind, you're about ready to go ahead. You have a lot of work – unpaid, non-writing work – to do.

● You should investigate joining the Author-Publisher Network – an association of enthusiastic and mutually supportive self-publishers. (See Checklist 33.)

There is just the one really good British book about self-publishing. It's written by a man who has been there, done it all and, for all I know, probably designed and published the T-shirts. Peter Finch has been an editor, a self-publisher, a bookseller, a commercially published poet and short-story writer – and a commercially-published, how-to writer. He knows.

His book, *How to Publish Yourself*, is in the same series as this book, published by Allison & Busby. If you intend to self-publish, get it. (Peter has also written the more specialist *How to Publish Your Poetry*, again, from Allison & Busby.)

82 Vanity publishers

'Proper' – mainstream – publishers assess the quality of any book which is offered to them and, if the book is then accepted, they (usually*) meet the full cost of publication and pay the author a proportion of the sales revenue (basically in royalties). The author is not required to make any financial contribution whatsoever to the production/publication process. The conventional publisher is in business: he makes a commercial judgement on the saleability of the

---

* Very occasionally, a mainstream publisher will take on an otherwise commercially unattractive book of narrow interest if part of the costs are met by an interested organisation – i.e., if the publication is subsidised. (A typical example might be the anniversary history of a major commercial firm.) NEVER though, suggest or agree if asked, to subsidise your own book – that's vanity publishing, see main text.

author's work. He makes his profit from the product of the book's sales less the full cost of the production (including author's royalties), distribution and marketing process.

Vanity publishers make their profits by publishing – usually in extremely small numbers – virtually anything they are offered, in exchange for an extremely large payment – a 'contribution' – by the author. They usually say that they are 'subsidy publishers'. (In an investigation by ardent campaigner Johnathon Clifford, the 'contribution' required by the 'publisher' was considerably in excess of the printing costs.)

- Any publisher advertising for authors (and/or poets) to submit their work for consideration for publication is 99.9 per cent certain to be a vanity publisher. (Conventional publishers are inundated with unsolicited submissions of books of all kinds. In general, less than 1 per cent of unsolicited *and* *'un-agented'* fiction manuscripts are accepted, and very few mainstream firms publish poetry at all.)
- A vanity publisher will respond quickly, praise your work and be eager to publish it. (Real publishers take time to consider your work.)
- Any publisher who asks *an author* for a 'contribution' towards the cost of publication is a vanity publisher. The 'contribution' is usually exorbitant.
- Few bookshops and even fewer public libraries will (knowingly) stock any book published by a vanity publisher.
- A vanity publisher will often offer – in a large and impressive-looking legal document – royalty rates markedly in excess of the 'industry standard' (7.5–8 per cent on paperback list price and 10 percent on hardback list price sales). Vanity publishers have been known to 'offer' 35–40 per cent royalties, but on infinitesimal sales. It is difficult to persuade a mainstream publisher to increase by even 1 or 2 per cent.
- An author's reputation will not be enhanced by publication by a vanity publisher – the reverse. Only the naive and gullible get caught. You have been warned. (Vanity publishing, as such, is often perfectly legal. You have every right to make a fool of yourself.)
- A vanity publisher will seldom make any significant effort to sell his published books – he's made his profit from the author's 'contribution'.

9

MONEY-MAKING MATTERS

- ■ The 'business' of writing

- ■ Self-promotion

- ■ An author's biog

- ■ Pen-names

- ■ Giving a talk

- ■ Hyping your book

- ■ Selling your own books

- ■ Rights

- ■ Points to watch in a book agreement

83 The 'business' of writing

If you're still struggling to sell your first story, article or book, then this checklist is not – YET – for you. But if you're over that hurdle, the sooner you start being *businesslike* the better.

- ● You need a system for recording each piece of work you send out – its title, where and when it's submitted, and the result. Start a system NOW: it's hard to backtrack in a year or so's time. (See Checklist 94.)
- ● You need a scrapbook. (See Checklist 8.)
- ● You need a system for keeping (financial) accounts. (See Checklist 95.)
- ● If you haven't yet invested in a word processor, do think seriously about it. One solution is to set aside all your writing earnings until

you have enough to buy one. Your first word processor doesn't need to be expensive.

- Remember to renew your typewriter or computer-printer ribbons frequently. Nothing looks more amateurish than faint typescript. (This is a non-problem with ink-jet or laser printers – they just stop printing when the ink runs out. Make sure you always have a spare.)
- You need some *businesslike* headed note-paper – plain and simple – your word processor will 'produce' and save this for you. (See Checklist 25.).
- Investigate buying your stationery (ribbons, ink cartridges, paper, envelopes, files, etc.) in bulk – it all keeps. Phone Viking (Freephone 0800 424444) for their catalogue. Their stuff's excellent – and the cheapest I've found.
- If a magazine requires an invoice, submit one. If you have not been paid by the due date, send a Statement of Account. (See Checklist 96.)
- Adopt a businesslike approach when contacting editors – both in writing and if phoning. (See Checklists 31 and 72.)
- Once you've sold a book, rather than a shorter piece of work, be sure to publicise both the book AND YOURSELF. (See Checklists 84 and 88.)

[WF]

84 Self-promotion

Writers who are 'household names' tend to get more work than do those of a more reclusive nature. Ways to become better known, even in a small way, include:

- If you have a book published, let your publisher know that you are available for radio – or, in your dreams, TV – interviews to publicise it. If your publisher is not notifying local radio stations of your book's publication, then let them know yourself, with a press release. But check with the publisher first. (See Checklist 88.)
- Again, if a book is published, write articles about the subject for specialist magazines; offer a copy of the book cover as an illustration. (Your publisher can let you have two or three cover-pulls.) Time your production and offer of the articles to match the book's publication date. Ask your publisher to provide two or three free

copies of your book to the magazine for giveaways or minor prizes.

- Let it be known that you are available to give talks or classes about your subject. (As a near-last resort, insert a small ad in the relevant specialist magazine announcing your availability.) For tips on talks, see Checklist 87. Ensure that your talk/class is well publicised.

- Make the most of your achievements – a prize in a national writing competition (even a short-listing if sufficiently prestigious, e.g., the Booker Prize), a first, tenth or twentieth book published, etc., particularly if you are 'extra' young, or a pensioner – and send out a press notice to local newspapers and specialist magazines about it. (Keep press notices short – about 200 words maximum – and write them in the third person. Include your name and phone number at the foot of the page, for more information.)

- Have copies of a (flattering) black-and-white photograph of yourself and a 'writer's biog' (see Checklist 85) readily available.

- Consider the *possibility* of a small launch party on publication of one of your books. Such a party might be particularly worthwhile if your book has some local significance. Most times though, such a party is likely to be pure self-indulgence. Weigh the cost against the likely benefits ... and call it off.

- Have business cards (I favour discreet ones) printed and bestow them on anyone of relevant consequence. Similarly, give complementary copies of your book to anyone who may be of later assistance to your writing career.

- Prepare a personal PR brochure: a single A4 sheet, folded twice, printed on both sides, possibly incorporating a picture of you and reproduction(s) of book covers, a brief biography and a note of any extra services you offer, such as talks. Either print it yourself as necessary, directly from the PC, or have a few printed at a time. Uses include handing out at talks, or to interviewers, and sending to new-to-you editors and publishers.

85 An author's biog

As you continue to write, there will often be requests for your biography (or biog). You are seeking an agent – you need to enclose a biog; you write a book – the publisher asks for a biog; you are to give a talk to a writers' group – the chairperson has to introduce you and asks for a biog. It's worth giving your biog some thought – now, before it's needed – and keeping it on file, updated regularly.

- Your writing biog will need to be between 50 and say 400 words, depending on the purpose. You will probably need to adjust or rewrite it (to fit the requested length and purpose) for each use but a good standard all-purpose length is about 250 words.
- Write your biog exclusively in the third person – 'Gordon Wells began writing in 19xx ...'
- Mention your special writing interests and specialisms and give the names of just a few – two or three is ideal – of any books. (If you feel the need to mention more than a few books, it is best to refer to them more generally without giving the actual titles – 'He has also written children's non-fiction about dinosaurs, inventions and outer space.') If you have also – or only – written articles, say something like 'He has contributed feature articles to various magazines including [name of the best-known or most important magazine]'.
- Restrict your biog to your writing career. Unless you write a lot about your 'day job', don't mention any qualifications or your profession. (But if you have, for instance, a specialised MA in Creative Writing, this might possibly be worth a mention.)
- Do not mention your membership of writing organisations such as the Society of Authors or the Crime Writers' Association. Depending on the purpose of the biog though, it will sometimes be appropriate – a biog for the use of the chairperson of a writers' group – to mention elected office in writing organisations. '... Chairman of Southern Writers Conference 19xx-y.' Do not include this information in a biog being sent to a publisher or other business organisation.
- If you are using your biog in connection with offering a 'straight' novel or non-fiction book, it might be unwise to mention the half dozen Harlequin Mills & Boon books you have written – they could count against you.
- Should you have won a *significant* (and relevant) writing prize/award (Trask, Booker, Smarties, Whitbread, etc.), or even a mention/short-list placing, of course mention this – but not your second prize in a small press magazine's poetry competition.
- If you have a brief and favourable quote about one of your books, include this in the biog – depending on the biog purpose.
- Do not lie, distort the facts or mislead the reader of your biog – but

be sure to present the best side of yourself. Make the most of your achievements. And don't shout about any failures.

For an example of a fairly brief writer's biog, see the back cover of this book.

86 Pen-names

Some writers use one or more pen-names – pseudonyms – sometimes expressed as *aka*, from the American, 'also known as'. There are several good reasons for using a pen-name – and some less-than-good. Valid reasons include:

● Your first novel was accepted and published by a publisher whose agreement required you to give him first refusal of your next (and next, and next) novel on similar terms to the first. And the terms agreed for your first novel were less than generous. (It is not unreasonable for a publisher to expect an author to stick with him – he may invest in publicising the first novel expecting to recoup the expenditure on subsequent novels. It is only a problem where a perhaps naive, first-time novelist has accepted poor terms.) In this situation, a pen-name is a way out: the first publisher is, supposedly, unaware of his lost writer.

● A writer produces many novels and the publisher thinks the author's name is becoming 'overexposed'. Possibly the publisher accepts further work from the writer but under a different name – or maybe won't accept more than so many books per year, entailing the writer taking his/her extra output elsewhere ... under a pen-name.

● A writer has made a name for books in one genre and wants to write in another. Fans of books in the first genre may be disturbed to find another book by the favourite author, written in a totally different style. (Imagine buying erotica-writer Dolly Daydream's new book and finding it was a slushy romance. Or vice-versa.) Many writers use different pen-names for different genres.

● A male writer offering work – particularly short stories – to women's magazines might be well advised to write from a woman's viewpoint ... and use a female pen-name.

● People in some 'day jobs' who write in their spare time and wish – or need – to keep their two lives separate will often adopt a pen-name. (A policeman writing crime novels for instance might find this embarrassing at work.)

- Writers of erotica almost always write under a pseudonym, for obvious and valid reasons. (The most prolific erotic novelist of all is someone called Anon.)

- Prolific writers of non-fiction articles are sometimes asked, by a grateful editor, to permit some of their features to appear under a pen-name. Too many articles in one issue by the same writer doesn't look good.

- All of the above are good and valid reasons for using a pen-name. Using a pen-name to hide your other-than-erotic writing activities from friends and relations, purely out of embarrassment is not a good reason. You should be proud of your work. If you are not, improve it so that you are. Writing is an honourable trade.

And a practical tip: when selecting a pen name, avoid a surname starting with A (or maybe B) or Y or Z. Each of these extremes can be either on the top shelf or near the floor in bookshops and thus less noticeable/accessible. Opt for a middle-of-the-alphabet initial, taking care that your chosen name is not the same as someone well-known (or you'll always be in their shadow). Don't choose too outlandish a name either, you want to be remembered, not laughed about.

87 Giving a talk

As you write more and more, you will – maybe – become better known. Possibly, you will be invited to 'give a talk'. To give an entertaining, witty, 'after dinner' talk requires a special 'performing' talent – and often attracts commensurate fees. But there are many more opportunities to give somewhat less demanding talks: to writers' groups and conferences, Rotary clubs, or W.I. meetings, for instance. Giving a talk need not be terrifying, and it offers you good publicity … and often, the chance to sell copies of your books. All you have to do is go about it the right way …

Before you say yes:

- Ask how big a group you will be addressing. (An audience of a hundred-plus is a bit – but only a bit – off-putting and you will need to prepare rather more carefully; six to thirty-odd, no problem.)

- Ask about the level of knowledge/experience of group members. (It's not easy giving a talk to people who all know more than you about your subject. And primary-school-kids are not the easiest audience either.)

● Ask how long you will be expected to talk for – and whether this includes time for questions.

● Ask if you can bring copies of your books to sell.

● Ask about the fee (and travelling expenses if the venue is far from your home). Don't work for nothing – every labourer is worthy of their hire. And remember, you will be away from your desk where you would, in theory at least, be doing productive work and earning money.

● Discuss the subject they want you to talk about – and, before saying yes, assure yourself that you can deliver. If, like me, you don't think you can give an 'entertaining' talk, only an 'educational' one, make this clear – and get the hirer's agreement.

● Arrange, if necessary and possible, for a parking space.

Between 'yes' and 'the day':

● Identify your purpose. What are you going to talk about: your collection or hobby, how you started, how you work or how to do it?

● Collect your content material – facts/thoughts/advice/anecdotes/ jokes – and decide on the importance of each item to your audience.

● Decide on a structure for your talk ("Tell 'em three things, three times", or "Ten steps to …") and arrange your content to fit.

● Prepare the notes from which you will speak. Little more than a few main headings will be enough for an informal talk to a small group; you will feel more confident when talking to a larger audience if you have more comprehensive notes. You know your subject so, whatever the audience, your talk will come across best if you expand on notes rather than reading a script *verbatim*. (With good notes, you will never be lost for words.)

● Practise the talk to your mirror – but only once or twice to check that it's about the right length. (If not, get more material, or mark items to be left out.) DON'T try to learn it *verbatim* or it will come across as wooden.

On the day:

● Arrive early. (Check the route before you set out.)

● Locate and check the room in which you are going to talk – try to avoid using PA equipment. You might even have to move the furniture around if it's not right for you.

● You are nervous. Don't worry. You'd be no good if you weren't. DON'T have a drink to steady your nerves – slurred words don't improve anyone's diction. Your nerves will disappear after the first minute or so, as you get into your stride.

● Stand up, speak up, look (first) at someone near the back and speak to them. You'll see from their face whether or not they can hear you. If not, speak a little louder but don't shout.

● Watch the time – I have a digital clock with huge numbers on the table in front of me – and adjust what you're saying to the time available. (That's the advantage of speaking from notes.)

● Don't over-run the time; if you finish early invite questions.

● At the end, if it seems appropriate, mention your book(s) – and hope for buyers.

88 Hyping your book

When your book comes out, your publisher may ask you to assist in the publicity campaign. This may entail book signings at various retail outlets, or appearing on local radio for an interview or to answer phone-in questions. Some first-timers are unnecessarily apprehensive about such activities.

● If vast crowds turn up at your bookshop to buy your book and have you sign it ... be thankful. More usually, you will sit and wait for a customer to arrive.

   ◆ Ask your friends to come in and 'rotate' a single book purchase and mock signature. That will save the exercise *looking* too much of a disaster.

   ◆ Take some important-looking writing work into the bookshop to occupy yourself.

   ◆ When a few 'real' customers do turn up, engage them in friendly conversation. They will (hopefully) be flattered and you'll have cemented a 'fanship'. And they'll have helped to pass the time.

   ◆ Be ready with a short standard 'salutation' to go with your signature. Make sure you spell the purchaser's name correctly – no one will take a 'spoiled' copy.)

● At the local radio station, come prepared with a copy of your book (of course) and a single sheet of paper (so that you don't rustle pages) containing a few relevant reminder-notes – what the book's about (in one sentence), advice for beginners, how long it took to write, where you got the idea from, how you come to know enough to write it, and suchlike.

- If you are doing a radio interview 'down the phone line' from home, shut yourself away with the phone, in a quiet room, just before the station is due to call. Warn others to leave you alone. Turn off your own radio. The station will often play the broadcast down the phone line to let you hear the lead-in.

- If your book is in any way contentious – prepare a one-sentence defensive comment about it and brief answers to a few predictable questions.

- With luck, the interviewer will tell you a few minutes in advance, how he/she intends to commence the interview – use those minutes to prepare your first response.

- Give full, expansive answers to 'good' questions: one of the basic requirements of a local radio interview is a change from the presenter's voice. What they DON'T want are monosyllabic responses; they want you to be interesting. Most times the interviewer will 'feed' you the right sort of questions: questions that 'invite' you to do well.

- Don't be worried about the possibly large audience out there listening: in reality, you are talking to a lot of one-person audiences. Talk therefore, as one to one. Try to talk fairly slowly – don't gabble (as I am prone to).

- Be as straightforward and unself-conscious as possible during the interview. Try to relax, and enjoy it. Remember too that the interviewer wants you to do well – it's his/her programme.

- Be sure to mention the title of your book at least once, and preferably more often – but without sounding too pushy. The interviewer will usually round off the session by a detailed reminder of the book's title, price and publisher.

- DO NOT have a drink to settle your nerves just before you arrive at the studio. It won't help and it may turn your first broadcast into a disaster.

89 Selling your own books

You've had a book published. You're over the moon. You've given copies to Mum, Dad and the boy/girl-friend. Don't give too many away though: freebies are always popular.

Now ... you can sell some. Writers' conferences often operate a book-room (taking around 10 per cent for conference funds), or maybe you have been asked to give a talk (see Checklist 87) and can sell copies of your book after that. (Your agreement will permit you to buy more copies of your book 'for your own use' at 35-40 per cent discount: publishers will usually turn a blind eye to 'your own use' selling. Don't buy too many at a time: you can always re-order. I seldom buy more than ten at one time.)

Some advice on selling your book:

- Display them as well as you can – lying flat on the table they are less visible than propped upright.
- If someone shows interest in the book, describe it – fairly and honestly.
- Offer – tentatively – to sign the book. Decide in advance whether you are going to just sign, or add a few words like, 'Best wishes'. (Anything too long will take up selling time.)
- Take a small 'float' of change with you. (It's sensible to make the float a round and memorable sum – say £10, in various coins. Don't bother about the odd pennies, people seldom insist on receiving the 1p change on a £8.99 book price – but the want of £1 could lose you the sale)
- Accept cheques – check amount and signature, but don't bother with cheque card guarantees.
- Make a note of how many books you have brought with you and check number sold against cash received.
- Don't neglect to record profits from book sales in your accounts. (You never know, you may have sold a book to a diligent tax inspector or his/her spouse.)

90 Rights

From the moment you commit your thoughts, ideas or facts into words on paper (or onto some form of electronic storage device such as a hard, or floppy disk) you own the copyright in them. (The copyright exists in the form in which you express your thoughts, ideas or facts – neither ideas nor facts can themselves be copyrighted.) You are then free to sell various rights in your work. Several points are worthy of attention.

- You write an article or short story and submit it to a magazine for publication. The magazine being a *serial* (i.e., not 'one-off') publication, you are offering *Serial Rights* in the work. If the magazine is published in Britain, you will usually be offering *British* Serial Rights. If the piece of writing has not already been published in Britain, you are offering *First* British Serial Rights (also referred to as FBSR).

• If the piece of work you are offering is an article, the offer of First British Serial Rights is assumed and you do not need to state this. Because the article will usually have been written to the specific requirements of the magazine, the *unchanged* article will almost certainly be unsuitable for offer elsewhere. But, there being no copyright in facts, there is nothing to stop you *rewriting* the article –with some differences in content – and again offering (unspecified but assumed) First British Serial Rights in the 'new' article. The same principle applies even if the magazine demands First Galaxy Serial Rights or even All Rights. (With All Rights, they are still only buying the copyright in that specific form of expression: the facts remain re-usable.)

• If the piece of work is a short story, short stories being a commodity that can sometimes be sold more than once without change, you need to specify, on the story's cover sheet (see Checklist 23), that you are offering *First British Serial Rights*. Once one magazine has published the story, if you offer it to another British magazine you must make it clear that you are offering *Second British Serial Rights*.

• If you now submit your once-sold short story to a, say, Scandinavian magazine, you can offer First *Scandinavian* Serial Rights. Similarly, First American, Australian, Chinese or Zimbabwean Serial Rights.

• It doesn't matter where your piece of written work, article or short story is published or whether or not you are paid for publication, you will have disposed of/released/relinquished *First* British Serial Rights. (If first publication was in a magazine of very limited circulation – a firm's house magazine, a club newsletter, etc. – a 'mainstream' magazine may be willing to accept it despite the absence of *First* Rights, but you must make its previous publication clear.)

• If you now write a book and wish to re-use your article therein – unchanged – or wish to include the short story in an anthology, you are free to do so. The publication in book form exercises *Book Rights*. (Some of the checklists in this book have already appeared in magazines.)

• Similarly, a short story may be read on the radio before or after it appears in a magazine; the broadcast uses *Broadcasting Rights* which do not conflict with *Serial* or *Book* Rights.

- When a book is offered to a publisher in Britain, he may expect World Book Rights. If the book is capable of being sold in America, an agent may withhold American Book Rights and sell these separately. (Few authors negotiate such deals themselves.)
- Some publishers 'buy' both hardback and paperback rights in your book – others will only take one or the other, leaving the remaining right available for later sale elsewhere. There are also translation rights, serial rights, book club rights, etc., even strip cartoon rights, all of which, in most cases, are best left to the publisher to handle on the author's behalf. The publisher sells one of the subsidiary rights and pays the author a percentage of what he gets – as specified in the agreement.
- Nowadays, there is increasing interest in Electronic Rights. The Society of Authors advises against relinquishing these without careful consideration.

91 Points to watch in a book agreement

Your novel has been accepted or you've got the go-ahead for that non-fiction book you've long wanted to write. The publisher will send you a contract – an agreement – to sign. The agreement is a longish legal document and the first sight is always a bit off-putting. First, some points to remember:

- ◆ Don't consult your local high street solicitor about the agreement – 'general practice' solicitors don't understand them and will start changing minor, unimportant aspects, while you run up a sizeable bill. Once you have a contract, you are eligible to join the Society of Authors (see Checklist 33) who will vet and advise members on their agreements free of charge.
- ◆ The agreement you receive will look final, but if you want any reasonable amendments, the publisher will usually discuss these with you and often make the changes you want.
- ◆ If you have an agent, he/she will already have vetted the agreement – it may in fact be the *agent's* standard agreement, imposed on the publisher.

The most important points to note/check in your agreement are:

- Author's warranties – are you sure that nothing in your book is libellous, obscene, blasphemous, etc.?

- Publisher's undertaking – has the publisher committed himself to publishing the book within a reasonable time (say 12 months) from your delivery of the complete typescript?

- Delivery of typescript – have you negotiated enough time for you to complete the book? It is up to you to deliver the complete book by the contracted date.

- Proofs – no problems here but do remember that PROOFS ARE FOR CORRECTION, NOT FOR RETHINKING. If you rewrite much you will be charged the cost of the changes – very little comes for free at this point.

- Licence period – if your book is of great commercial importance have you negotiated a limited period only? (For most books, a variation in the 'standard' period of copyright is not justified.)

- Royalties and advances – broadly speaking, you can expect royalties of 7.5 per cent (paperbacks) and 10 per cent (hardbacks) on home sales at list price and an advance of perhaps half the product of the first print run (some authors get much more). Look for a royalty jump of perhaps 2.5 per cent after sales of 3,000 (hardback), 10,000 (trade paperback) or 25,000 (mass market paperback). If royalties are to be based on publisher's receipts, you need about double the list price royalty rate, to compensate for big discounts.

- Subsidiary rights – are you satisfied that you (or your agent) have safeguarded the subsidiary rights – or that it is wise to allow the publisher to retain and look after them?

- Royalty statements and payment dates – most publishers provide statements and payments at six-monthly intervals, specified in the agreement.

- Remaindering – if the book is remaindered (i.e., unsold copies sold off at around production cost), is there provision for you to be warned, and to acquire copies at the remainder price?

- Free copies – nowadays, many publishers give authors a dozen free copies of a hardback book and 20 of a paperback, on publication and further copies on each new edition. If only offered six or less – past practice – it's worth a try, asking for more.

- Termination of agreement – is there a clause allowing for the rights in the book to revert to the author if it is allowed to go out of print? (You should ALWAYS claim back your rights if the book stays O/P.)

- Option on author's next book – for non-fiction, ask for this to be qualified 'in a similar field'; for fiction, ponder on the terms being offered.

10

THE BOTTOM LINE

- **What do they pay?**

- **Negotiating payment rates**

- **Recording magazine submissions**

- **Keeping financial records**

- **Invoices**

- **Collecting late money**

- **Income Tax and National Insurance**

92 What do they pay?

Writing is hard work. We should not be doing it without appropriate payment. Some editors (and publishers) prefer not to put all their financial cards on the table – they need 'room' to negotiate. At the same time, novice writers need to have some idea of what payment their work is likely to attract. In VERY BROAD TERMS, therefore:

- One-hundred-word, paying 'letters to editors' can earn anything from £3 to £25 with an average of about £10 and the 'star' letter earning maybe two or three times the standard.
- Articles in county-type magazines, specialist magazines, and the lower-paying women's magazines are usually paid at about £30-50 per 1,000 words.
- The newspaper weekend supplements, the top women's magazines and some up-market specialist magazines usually pay £100 and more per 1,000 words, for 'quality' articles.
- Short-short stories (around 1,000 words) will earn £50-100 in the lower-paying women's magazines, and £200-plus in the top-paying women's magazines.

145

- 'Traditional' short stories – i.e., around 2,000 words – can attract £100-500.
- A first novel could attract an advance (against future royalties) of £500-1,500.
- A genre novel will often attract an advance of £1,000-2,000. (But in some genres, some publishers offer only £300.)
- A genre novel from an experienced and 'known' author could attract an advance of £5,000 or more – and possibly a contract for several books at a time.
- A how-to non-fiction book will often attract an advance of £300-500 – but some publishers are even offering zero advances. A how-to book – or any other narrowly specialist non-fiction book – will seldom be offered more than a £1,000-1,500 advance.
- A general-interest non-fiction book might well attract an advance of £1,000 ... and much more depending on the subject and author.
- A children's non-fiction book might be offered a lump sum (flat) fee of £500-1,000.
- Royalties for all books (fiction and non-fiction) are usually 10 per cent of list price for hardbacks, 7.5 per cent of list price for trade paperbacks and anywhere between 3 and 8 per cent for mass market paperbacks. (If the royalties offered are to be based on a percentage of publishers' net receipts, all these rates should be *about* doubled – to compensate for massive discounts.

93 Negotiating payment rates

Many writers don't like to discuss payment with their editors and publishers. 'It's not the done thing, to talk about money.' You may think that some people are too 'up front' when it comes to money but it is helpful for a little of that attitude to rub off. Remember you are in business. You are offering something unique to the marketplace.

Where there is room for price/payment negotiation, buyers will usually start with a low offer; you can sometimes get more. Try this approach:

- When dealing with magazine editors and book publishers alike, avoid specifying how much you expect to be paid – let them make the opening offer.
- Financial negotiations are best made face to face across a table or – more likely – on the phone: exchanging letters takes too long and both parties want a quick decision.

- If a magazine editor doesn't tell you how much (and when) you are to be paid for an article or short story ... ask him/her.

- Maybe with your first (or first few) acceptances, you are anxious to avoid rocking the boat – your only objective is acceptance and publication. OK, that's understandable. Once you have a bit more confidence though, you can NEARLY ALWAYS ask for more. (After all: the editor can easily say 'No' – to the extra.) But remember that sometimes, the rate you are offered is what your work is worth.

- Once the editor quotes you a figure, say something like, 'I was hoping for rather more than that. How about [suggest a figure perhaps 20 per cent higher]?' If the editor says he can't go as high as that, and offers 5 per cent more, suggest a compromise of, say, 10 per cent up. Be ready to accept whatever figure you can get. (You can always try for more next time.) Also be prepared to be told that this is a standard rate and that no increase is possible: this is frequently the case.

- As soon as you and the editor have agreed a payment figure, confirm it to him/her in a letter the same day: also confirm what you will be supplying and the agreed delivery date.

- When negotiating with a book publisher, payment is usually a matter of royalties and advances. For most books, most authors, a royalty of 10 per cent on the published list price of a hardback and 7.5-8 per cent of a paperback are fairly standard for 'general list' books. (Lower rates often apply to education books and some mass-market paperbacks.) The need for negotiating is more likely to arise if you are offered a royalty based on the publisher's net receipts. (With retailers demanding discounts of 50 per cent or more, the royalty rate should be at least doubled if based on net receipts. Some publishers try for less.) Apply the same principles as outlined above.

- Publishers' advances are a movable feast: they will offer a big name author a huge advance, more than is likely to be earned from the royalties, to keep the name in their list. Offers to lesser authors are much much less. Expect/hope for a total advance equal to the product of half the initial print run. Ask for more money if you are offered less than these figures. (As a guide, a print run of 2,000-3,000 copies is not uncommon for first novels or general non-fiction books.)

- There will often be a royalty increase (a royalty 'jump') in your agreement; this is frequently pitched at such a high level of sales that it is most unlikely ever to be reached. Negotiate for a lower sales figure for the 'jump'.

- In all financial negotiations, move tentatively and trust your instincts. You would have to be most unfortunate to lose a sale/acceptance merely by *asking* for more money. Remember: those who don't ask, don't get.

94 Recording magazine submissions

As you produce more, the need for keeping tags on your work increases. Unless you keep a record of which article or short story you have sent to which magazine and when, you can get into a muddle. Potentially, you could resubmit the same piece to a magazine that has already rejected it. Equally, you wouldn't necessarily know where a particular piece of work is at any time. How long have they had it; has it been published; when are they likely to pay you?

Articles are usually written for a specific market and if rejected are rewritten for another. Short stories are written once and are potentially saleable to more than one magazine. So slightly different record systems are recommended:

For short stories

Use a separate page (actual or electronic, within your word processor) for each story, headed with the story title and a note of its length. List each submission under the following column heads:

- Magazine to which submitted (usually initials only)
- Date submitted (For convenience, I convert all dates into a single six-figure number, thus, 23 March 1999 becomes 230399.)
- Decision (A, accepted; R, rejected)
- Decision date (as above)
- Publication date – and tick if and when magazine copy received
- Payment (£)
- Payment date (as above)

For articles

Start a fresh page (actual or electronic) each year. List each article submitted – one line per submission – under the following column heads:

- Item number (I number each piece of work, from 1, throughout the year.)
- Computer file name (To save space, I stick to the old MS-DOS 8-character file-name and also differentiate between articles [A], picture-scripts [S], etc.)
- Abbreviated article title (in case the filename is difficult to 'translate')
- Length, and number of illustrations (E.g., 900/2 means 900 words and 2 pix)
- ... then, following that, the same columns as above – from Magazine to Payment date.

If an article is rejected then the last three columns – Publication date to Payment date – provide space for details of any alternative submission, below.

For books

Less necessary, because you are unlikely to have many books on offer at the same time. Keep a note of which publishers you have approached with which book and on what date – so that you know when to chase them for a response.

95 Keeping financial records

You will need to keep check on how much you are earning from your writing activities, for your own information. You may also – depending on how much you earn from your writing (see Checklist 98) – need to be able to show your accounts to the tax inspectors. (However small your earnings though, don't forget that you MUST declare them. If you neglect to declare them, be sure your sins will eventually be found out: magazines and publishers have to report payments to writers, to the tax authorities.)

Your accounts need not be very complicated nor an onerous task to keep up. Basically, all you need do is record all receipts and all associated expenses. (You should also keep receipts for any significant items of expenditure.) When you are starting you can manage with the simplest possible cash book and merely record each receipt on one half of a double-page spread and the more numerous items of expenditure on the opposite page. Start each month afresh – but keeping totals running – with either a line across the page or a fresh page.

As you spend and earn more on your writing, you will probably wish to record a detailed breakdown of the expenditure – this saves time later when preparing a breakdown of expenditure in the year-end accounts. I use an analysis book with 14 cash columns. I use the first two cash columns to record simple receipts and expenses; in the rest of the columns I REPEAT the expenditure, broken down by type (postage, travel, etc.) Because receipts are relatively few, I use a small column adjacent to the receipts column to mark their source – articles, books, talks, etc. – and separate them out at the year-end.

My own expenditure breakdown columns are as follows – you might use similar headings:

- Postage (charged as posted, not when stamps are bought)
- Research (including relevant magazine subscriptions)
- Stationery (including film and processing – and many printer cartridges)
- Travel (actual cost or car mileage, currently charged at 10p per mile)
- Book purchases (my own books, for sale to others)
- Outgoing telephone calls and fax expenses (I also 'charge up' the telephone rental)
- Conference attendance fees
- Relevant subscriptions (currently Society of Authors and London Writer Circle)
- Odds (a *small* computer program, perhaps)
- Allowance for use of study. (The tax inspector accepts a claim of £120 per year from me. Take care: if you seek to charge a proportion of total house running expenses based on room size or suchlike, and can persuade the tax inspector to accept this, you may have Capital Gains Tax problems if and when you come to sell your house. Much better to stick to *partial* use of the room, which has no CGT connotations.)

Separately, for tax purposes, you should record capital expenditure: new computer, printer, fax machine, etc. Under current tax regulations, you can treat a percentage of the capital expenditure as an annual expense to set against the income. (Currently, you can allow 25 per cent of the initial cost of, say, £1,000 as current expenditure; the balance of £750 is carried forward to the next tax year and then, again, 25 per cent *of that balance*, i.e., £187.50, can be treated as current expenditure. You are also required to set off any receipts from the sale of old equipment against the replacement cost.)

96 Invoices

Some writers worry unnecessarily when asked to supply an invoice. An invoice is no more than a request for payment.

- Use a sheet of your business (i.e., headed) notepaper or type your name and address at the top of a sheet of plain A4 paper.
- Centrally, a few lines down from the heading/address, type INVOICE (in caps).
- A few more lines down, at the left margin, type the name and address of the firm to which the invoice is to be submitted. (For book-related invoices, the name of the publisher, not that of the editor or person you normally deal with, within the publishing house. For magazine invoices, the name of the magazine-publisher rather than the editor.)
- Two or three more lines down, at left margin, the date. (If possible, be prepared to adjust line spacings later – see below.)
- Two or three more lines down, at left margin, repeat the word INVOICE. You may decide to number all your invoices in sequence: if so, range to right margin and type in 'Invoice No: 000' on this same line. (I don't issue many invoices: for me the date suffices.)
- Two or three more lines down, at left margin, type 'To:'
- Two more lines down and detail the product, work or service for which you are billing the invoice recipient. (Mention the name of the magazine or the book to which the invoice relates.) Do not extend these 'details' lines more than about two-thirds of the way across to the right margin.
  - ◆ Within the details block, include the title of the article or story and the date of the magazine-issue in which it appears or the date of the acceptance letter.
  - ◆ On the last line of the details block, type a row of dots (or two dots, two spaces, two dots, etc.) and close to the right margin, type the amount being billed. (If you don't know how much you are to be paid for an article or story, leave the amount blank – the editor will put it in.)
  - ◆ If billing a publisher for an advance, ensure that it is clear which portion of the advance is being invoiced – 'on signa-ture', 'on delivery', or 'on publication'.

- If you are billing for more than one item or service on the same invoice, repeat (but with different information, of course) the detail-block and amount due.
  - ◆ Use a separate 'details block' for each article/story/etc. in one issue of the magazine; a further separate one for any pre-agreed expenses.
- Two or three lines beneath the amount(s) due, inset an inch or so from left margin, type, in caps, TOTAL AMOUNT DUE, and, beneath the individual figures, insert the total amount of the invoice.
- Centrally, a few lines beneath the TOTAL line, in brackets, state 'Not registered for VAT' or 'VAT registration No. ...'
- If using a word processor to produce the invoice, at this stage, check the layout and adjust line spacings as necessary to improve the overall appearance of the invoice – centrally on a single page.
- Make two copies of the invoice: send one to the editor or person you have been dealing with, for authorising and forwarding to the relevant accounts section; retain and file one copy yourself. When paid, annotate the file copy.
- Check your file of invoices regularly for accounts outstanding and draw the attention of the publisher's accounts section to the delayed payments.

It is also useful, having issued several invoices to a single (magazine/book) publisher, to submit a monthly Statement of Account. For this, again use headed notepaper and address the firm not the individual. Head it Statement of Account and list (in tabular form, separating individual magazine titles, books and unrelated services) invoices issued by date, magazine issue, title and amount due. Break the tables to show, separately, invoices paid during previous month and invoices still due. Make two copies: despatch one and file the other.

97 Collecting late money

We writers are worthy of our hire. We should be paid. Sometimes though, some magazines and some publishers get behind with payments. What can we do?

- Phone the accounts section of a magazine or publisher and POLITELY enquire the position – maybe their routine is to pay at a specific time after publication, or maybe only on receipt of an invoice ... and nobody told you of this.

● Send an invoice (probably best, through the editor, for confirming). If payments continue to fall behind, I would submit regular invoices with each piece of work, even if they are not specifically required – and always keep copies of invoices.

● At the end of each month, send a Statement of Account showing details of the amounts outstanding. (See Checklist 96.)

● If payments continue to fall further behind, or remain unpaid, write formally to the Managing Editor (or some such title – check the magazine's masthead or the publishers' catalogue for the most appropriate senior figure) inviting their early attention to the accounts. Send the letter by recorded delivery.

● By now, you should be considering offering no further work to this magazine or publisher. Write them off your list of markets.

● If there is still no response from the management, write again, advising that you will be taking action in the Small Claims Court.

The Small Claims Court:

◆ Identify your nearest County Court (in the Phone Book).

◆ Ask the Court for three copies (one for you, two for the Court) of form N1 (the Default Summons Form).

◆ Complete and return the simple form, with the court fee of 10 per cent of the amount claimed. (If you win, the cost of the fee is added to your claim.)

◆ The case is heard by a district judge, informally, in private, with no other lawyers present.

◆ If you win, the magazine or publisher will usually pay up immediately – but if they don't, collection of the debt can be both difficult and expensive. You may have to give it up at this stage.

● Throughout, if you belong to one of the professional writers' associations, you should consult them ... and be helped.

98 Income Tax and National Insurance

As soon as you start earning any money from your writing, you become a self-employed person and are liable to pay tax and, the oft-forgotten, National Insurance contributions on your earnings. It is best not to be too specific about payment rates, eligibility levels, etc. because the Chancellor of the Exchequer is prone to vary these from year to year in the Budget. There are, however, certain procedures that are likely to remain standard.

First of all, there are several helpful – and necessary – booklets available, for the asking, from your local office of the Contributions Agency (part of the D.S.S.). Find their number in the Phone Book; ask them for these free booklets:

CWL1   *Starting your own business?*
CWL2   *National Insurance contributions for self-employed people: Class 2 and Class 4*
CA 02 *National Insurance contributions for self-employed people with small earnings.*

Phone your local Tax Office too – in the phone book under Inland Revenue – for a (free) copy of: **IR104** *Simple tax accounts.*

Subject to your own checking in the above booklets – because like the rates, application levels, etc., the procedures too can be varied from time to time – you need to work through these steps:

● As soon as you start to make money at your writing – no matter how little – you should tell your local Tax Office, the Contributions Agency and Customs and Excise (for VAT) that you are starting up in business. The way to do this is to complete and submit just one single form, CWF1, which is included in booklet CWL1 (above). The one form covers all the Government agencies concerned.

● Keep account of all your writing earnings and related expenditure. You will have to submit details of your writing income and pay Income Tax on it. You will need to submit a self-assessment form each year to declare your income. If your total (gross) writing earnings are less than about £15,000 per year, you will not have to provide detailed accounts for taxation purposes: a simple three-line summary – Receipts/Less Expenditure/Net Earnings – will suffice.

● Note that, if you buy yourself a new computer, to use as a word processor, or some other piece of relevant equipment, you can set off a percentage (currently 25 per cent) of the capital cost as an expense against your annual writing income. You carry forward the residual capital cost to the following year and can then set off a further percentage (again, currently 25 per cent) of the 75 per cent 'carried forward cost' (i.e. 25 per cent of 75 per cent, which is 18.75 per cent of the original cost) against that following year's income. And the next year a further 25 per cent – of the by then 56.25 per cent residue of the original.

- If you are a woman aged under 60 or a man under 65 and self-employed (even if only part- or spare-time and even if you have other employment) you still have to pay Class 2 National Insurance (NI) contributions. The only exception is if you obtain a Certificate of Small Earnings Exception, or a formal letter from the Contributions Agency stating that you do not need the Certificate.

- If the net earnings from your self-employed writing are not expected to be more than about £3,500 per year (check this figure particularly, it varies annually) you should apply for the Certificate of Small Earnings Exception. To apply, complete and submit form CF10 which is included in booklet CA 02 (above). If granted, you won't have to pay NI contributions on your writing earnings. The Certificate has to be renewed annually: the Agency will remind you at the appropriate time.

- If your annual writing earnings are even smaller – the current limiting figure is eight hundred pounds – AND you are paying Class 1 NI contributions in a full-time job while writing in your spare time, you should still apply on form CF10. In this situation though, you will be told by the Contributions Agency that you do not need a Certificate. This letter remains valid until your earnings rise above the limit: it does not require annual renewal. But it's up to you to keep an eye on your earnings: if they rise above the limit, you should notify the Agency to that effect.

- Once your net annual writing income rises above the Exception Certificate limit, you will have to pay Class 2 NI contributions. These are currently just over £6 per week and they can be paid by monthly direct debit or quarterly against a bill.

- Once your net annual writing income rises still further and exceeds a profit level which is set annually in the Budget you will ALSO have to pay Class 4 NI contributions – currently at 6 per cent per annum – on your net income between that profit level and an upper limit. The relevant lower and upper profit levels are currently set at just over £7,000, and just over £24,000. And remember, this Class 4 contribution is in addition to the weekly Class 2 contribution. (The bad news is that the demand for the Class 4 NI contribution comes with the annual Income Tax demand; the good news is that once your writing income exceeds the aforementioned upper level, you don't have to pay any further NI contributions.)

- If your annual (gross, i.e., before deducting expenses) writing earnings exceed about £50,000, you will have to register for, and pay Value Added tax (VAT). In that case, you should also be employing the services of an accountant – and not bothering with this part of this book. It is possible to register for VAT if your earnings are less than the specified level. In some self-employment occupations this is a wise move, because you can claim back the VAT charged on purchases. For writers, low-turnover optional VAT registration is seldom sufficiently financially advantageous to justify the extra accounting work entailed.

99 Glossary

There are many 'trade' terms used in the writing business that may confuse the beginner. This glossary will help.

A4	Paper size – 297 x 210 mm.
Advance	A payment to an author, made before or at publication, being an advance against expected future royalty earnings. It has to be recouped from earnings from royalties before further payments are made.
Advertorial	A feature article which, to a degree covertly, enthuses about a commercial product – and is paid for by the commercial firm concerned.
Agent (Literary)	Someone who acts for client writers, placing their work with suitable publishers and negotiating terms.
Agony column	A regular magazine column answering or offering advice on readers' queries or problems.
Agreement	The contract between publisher and author.
aka	'also known as' – a pen-name or pseudonym.
Anecdote	A short account of a real-life incident relevant to and illustrating some aspect of the associated feature article.
Appendix	Part of a book but of less importance than the main text – printed at the back of the book, i.e., *appended*.
Back list	Already published books which are still in print.
Back story	Things that happened before the start of the story proper.
Bibliography	A list of books consulted by an author in his/her research. A stand-in for a specific acknowledgement.
Biography	A factual account of someone's life (or part life) researched and written by someone else. (Autobiography – a biography written

by the subject.)

Blurb   The promotional text, outlining – possibly exaggerating – the content of the book. Appears on the back cover of a paperback and usually on the inside of the hardback jacket.

Bodice-ripper   A sexy romance novel, often in an historical setting.

Book packager   A company that initiates a book project, commissions writers, etc., and funds it until it is a viable, often lavish, 'ready-to-publish' project – and then sells the complete package to a conventional/mainstream publisher. Packaged books are often designed to sell to several publishers, each in different countries, making the often-necessary large colour print run viable. Involved creative people are usually paid a (good) flat fee – no royalties.

Bullets   Usually large black dots used (but can be ticks, or squares, for example) to identify important items in a list. (Whereas a numbered list suggests a sequence or order of importance, bullets do not have this connotation.)

By-line   The name of the writer – usually immediately following the title.

Caption   The identification and descriptive material printed adjacent to an illustration.

Cliché   A hackneyed and over-used word, phrase, idea or plot.

Coffee table book   A book designed to look good on the coffee table – lavish, much-illustrated … little read.

Commissioned work   Work 'ordered' by a magazine or publisher – but quite possibly the idea having been previously offered by a writer – and, subject perhaps to an acceptable synopsis/outline, for which a contract is given.

Confession story   Not much used today, but a popular story form of the 1960s being a 'true-to-life', rather than factual, story written in the first person. The *formula* was 'sin, suffer and repent'.

Critique   A detailed analysis of someone's writing aimed at assessing and improving its potential for success. An unfortunate Americanism in increasing use in Britain. Even worse, it is sometimes used as a verb, *to critique*.

Deadline   The date by which material must be delivered.

Double-spacing   Type a line, miss a line. Does NOT refer to the spacing of words or characters within the line.

Double-page spread   Two facing pages of a book, designed as an entity.

Edition   All the copies of a book printed without significant change to the text and in one binding. Thus, there could be two identical hardback and paperback editions; the correction of a few typographical errors or minor updatings some while after publication would not warrant being classed as a new edition; the rewriting of a chapter, say, would. There can be several reprints within a single edition. A new edition should always have a new ISBN.

End matter   Those parts of a book which are printed after the main text – appendices, bibliography, index, etc.

Exposition   Explanation of and commentary on events, actions and characters' feelings in a novel. ('Telling', rather than 'showing'.)

Faction   Fact written as fiction.

FBSR   First British Serial Rights – the right to publish a piece of written work for the first time in a British magazine.

Filler   A short piece of writing, in Britain seldom more than 400 words (longer in America) used to fill up the space at the end of an article. Can be humour, anecdote, odd facts, even verse.

Flashback   A device used, mainly in fiction, to bring in a back story.

Folio	A manuscript page.
Freebie	Slang expression for giveaway copies of a book or magazine.
Galley proof	A proof print of a book's text, not yet divided up into pages, and with neither illustrations, nor spaces for illustrations. (Seldom used nowadays.)
Genre	A literary category, such as romance, western, crime, thriller, etc.
Ghost (writer)	Someone who writes for, or in conjuction with, another as if the work were written by the other. The ghost may not get a credit.
Graphic novel	A full 'novel-length' story told in pictures (as in comics).
Hook	The opening words, sentences or paragraphs in a piece of work, which grab the reader's attention and tempt him to read on.
House style	The punctuation, spelling, layout, etc., used consistently by a publisher or magazine. (E.g., *ise* or *ize*, *word processor* or *word-processor*.)
Imposition	The arrangement of a book or magazine's pages on a large sheet of paper, so that once printed and folded, the pages are in the correct sequence.
ISBN (International Standard Book Number)	The unique number which, for each book, identifies the country (or broader area) of publication, the publisher and the book. (See back cover and page iv of this book.)
Justified typesetting	The spacing of words and characters so that each line of text is the same length, flush at both left and right – as in a book – rather than flush left only as in unjustified typescript.
Kill fee	A fee paid by a magazine when commissioned or accepted work is not then used. The kill fee is usually less than the full fee. Similarly, publishing firms often pay an 'on signature' advance well before delivery/publication of a non-fiction book: if an acceptable work is not then published, it is customary for the author to retain the

Literal

Manuscript

Masthead

MTA (Minimum
Terms Agreement)

Novella

On spec

OP

Orphan

Outline

Page proofs

Pen-name
Pic/pix
Picture-script

advance – and often to be paid the rest of the contracted advance.

(Increasingly known by the American term, *typo*.) A typing or typesetter's error.

(Abbreviation: MS – in caps, no full stops – plural MSS.) The meaning is handwritten work; in practice the expression is now virtually interchangeable with *typescript* – and is usually the product of a word processor.

Either a magazine's title format or, more often, the list of the magazine's staff and their titles, usually found near the contents page of a magazine or tucked away at the back.

The Society of Authors and the Writers' Guild of Great Britain have negotiated (relatively) standard terms of agreement with an increasing number of British publishers.

A short novel. There is no laid down length but as a guide, perhaps between 15,000 and 30,000 words. Don't hope to sell one nowadays.

Unsolicited work submitted speculatively for consideration for publication by a magazine or publisher.

A book trade abbreviation for *out of print*.

A single first line of a paragraph at the foot of a page. (See also *Widow*.)

An advance summary of the content of a proposed article: usually includes title, hook paras and a bullet-point list of further items.

The proofs of a book set out in page format as they will appear in the book. (There should be appropriate blank spaces for any not-yet-available illustrations thereby maintaining the correct pagination.)

A writer's pseudonym. (*See also* aka.)

Journalists'/publishers' slang for picture(s).

The written material for a story (including non-fiction) told in a sequence of drawn or photographic pictures, as in comics. The

Plagiarism

script consists of artist's briefing, dialogue and thoughts (to be displayed in speech balloons and thought-bubbles), sound effects (SFX) and any necessary captions.

The unauthorised, unacknowledged use – without direct copying, which would be an infringement of copyright – of another writer's work.

PLR (Public Lending Right)

An annual payment compensating registered authors for borrowings of their books from public libraries.

Prelims (Preliminary pages)

The pages of a book preceding the main text; in non-fiction books they usually follow a standardised format – see Checklist 48.

Proof correction marks

Standard signs used in the correction of proofs.

Protagonist

The main or lead character in a story.

Quotes

An abbreviation for the punctuation marks – inverted commas – used at each end of speech or other quoted material. Present-day practice is to use single quotes for most purposes and double-quotes only for quotations-within-quotations. Some older publishers adopt the reverse practice for their house style.

Remainder

To release warehouse space and/or ease cash flow, publishers often sell leftover stocks of books to specialist remainder merchants at a very low price (usually less than 10 per cent of list price), who then resell the books through discount bookshops. Authors' agreements should give the author the first opportunity to buy stocks at the remaindered price.

Reprint

A second or further print run of a book – without significant alteration to the text. (Significant changes are the criterion for a *Revised Edition*.)

Royalty

The payment made by a publisher to an author in respect of each copy sold, based on an agreed percentage of the book's list price or on the publisher's receipts for the book.

SAE

Stamped (self-) addressed envelope. (In

American terminology, SASE – for self-addressed stamped envelope.)

Shout line   The explanatory and complimentary comment on the front cover of a paperback that encourages potential purchasers. NOT the sub-title.

Side-bar   A short supplement to a feature article: additional related information, contacts, etc. – usually in a box on the same page(s) as the associated article. (Long favoured in American magazines, fast increasing in popularity in Britain.)

Slush pile   The large amount of unsolicited material, mostly unsuitable, received in a magazine or publisher's office.

Standfirst   Introductory material, in a magazine, separate from the article or short story which follows. For short stories, sometimes called a 'taster'.

Synopsis   A much-condensed version of the content of a book. For a non-fiction book, often a series of brief within-chapter headings; for a novel, the full story-line (introducing the main characters and always including any denouement).

Theme   The concept underlying a story. (E.g., 'crime doesn't pay'.)

Trade paperback   A paperback book unlikely to sell in the huge quantities required of a mass-market paperback. Better produced – and more expensive – than a mass-market paperback, often also has a larger page-size. (This present book is a trade paperback.)

'Twist in the tail' story (Or 'twister'.)   A short story whose ending, while logical, is unexpected.

Voucher copy   A copy of a magazine sent free of charge to a writer whose work is in it – to *vouch* for the work's appearance.

Widow   A single (and short makes it worse) last line of a paragraph appearing at the head of a fresh page. (*See also* orphan.)

My thanks to Chriss McCallum for letting me 'borrow' extensively from her comprehensive *Glossary for Writers*. (£3.50 post paid, from her at PO Box 96, Altrincham, Cheshire WA14 2LN.)

INDEX